NEEDS ASSESSMENTS IN PUBLIC POLICY

NEEDS ASSESSMENTS IN PUBLIC POLICY

Edited by
Janie Percy-Smith

Open University Press
Buckingham · Philadelphia

Open University Press
Celtic Court
22 Ballmoor
Buckingham
MK18 1XW

and
1900 Frost Road, Suite 101
Bristol, PA 19007, USA

First Published 1996

A catalogue record of this book is available from the British Library

ISBN 0 335 19595 4 (pb)   0 335 19596 2 (hb)

Library of Congress Cataloging-in-Publication Data
Needs assessments in public policy/Janie Percy-Smith, ed.
    p.   cm.
Includes bibliographical references and index.
ISBN 0–335–19596–2 (hb). – ISBN 0–335–19595–4 (pb)
1. Human services – Evaluation.   2. Social planning.
3. Needs assessment.   4. Needs assessment – Case studies.
I. Percy-Smith, Janie.
HV40.N4277   1996
361'.0068'4 – dc20   95–43060
                                                                                      CIP

Typeset by Type Study, Scarborough
Printed in Great Britain by St Edmundsbury Press, Bury St Edmunds, Suffolk

CONTENTS

LIST OF CONTRIBUTORS

Allan Blake is Deputy Dean of the Faculty of Business, Leeds Metropolitan University. He was a member of the Legal Aid Board from 1988 to 1993.

Martin Browne is a Senior Policy Analyst at the Policy Research Institute, Leeds Metropolitan University, where he is engaged in local needs auditing and the development of computer software for conducting community profiles. He was formerly Senior Planning and Information Officer at Bradford City Council Social Services Department.

Professor Mike Campbell is Director of the Policy Research Institute. He has undertaken extensive research on labour market needs for training and enterprise councils and the Department for Education and Employment and has advised the Sri Lankan government on the development of a labour market information system. He is co-editor of *Local Labour Markets: Problems and Policies* (Longman, 1992).

Anne Foreman is a Policy Analyst at the Policy Research Institute, Leeds Metropolitan University, where she is currently involved in a research project examining collaboration in the fields of housing, health and social care. She has, in the past, worked for a number of health authorities undertaking research into community care, hospital discharge procedures and lifestyles.

Murray Hawtin is a Senior Policy Analyst at the Policy Research Institute, Leeds Metropolitan University, where he undertakes research and consultancy in the area of social housing. He has formerly worked for the Department of Housing, Leeds City Council, on an estate pioneering a locally based approach to housing management. He is co-author of *Health, Housing and Social Policy* (Socialist Health Association, 1993), *Community Profiling: Auditing Social Needs* (Open University Press, 1994) and is currently co-editing a book on Tenants' Participation to be published by Avebury Press.

Dr Janie Percy-Smith is Principal Policy Analyst at the Policy Research Institute, Leeds Metropolitan University, where she is responsible for coordinating and developing research and consultancy in the fields of social auditing, community profiling and needs assessment. She is co-author of *Understanding Local Needs* (IPPR, 1992) and *Community Profiling: Auditing Social Needs* (Open University Press, 1994).

David Porteous is a Research Officer at the Policy Research Institute, Leeds Metropolitan University, where he is involved in a wide range of research activities in the fields of community needs, training and education, labour markets and the labour process, and information and communication technologies.

Dr Ian Sanderson is Principal Policy Analyst at the Policy Research Institute, Leeds Metropolitan University, where he coordinates research and consultancy activities in relation to evaluation and public services. He was formerly Head of the Policy Planning Unit at Fife Regional Council. He is editor of *Management of Quality in Local Government* (Longman, 1992) and co-author of *Understanding Local Needs* (IPPR, 1992).

PART I

THEORETICAL, CONTEXTUAL AND METHODOLOGICAL ISSUES

1 JANIE PERCY-SMITH

INTRODUCTION: ASSESSING NEEDS. THEORY AND PRACTICE

Introduction

This collection of papers takes as its starting point a strong belief that meeting needs is what public services ought to be about. This is clearly a normative statement which is reflective of my own political values, but it is also empirically rooted. It is the case, as a matter of fact, that need, variously and often imperfectly defined, is the basis on which a range of public services are currently distributed, as will become clear from the case study chapters in Part II of this volume. This is reflected in policy statements and statements of intent across policy areas. It is also true to say that, for ordinary people, the concept of need is often inextricably tied up with issues of fairness and social justice. So people react with outrage to stories of scarce public resources going to people who are not 'really' in need or of people in 'real need' going without. Although this can also be used as the basis for emotive attacks on 'scroungers' and those who are deemed to be undeserving in a moral sense of public assistance, it does nevertheless reflect a common acceptance that the concept of need is, and should be, an important consideration in decisions about the allocation of public resources. It is interesting to note that this appears to continue to be the case despite 15 years or more of ideological attack on need as the basis of provision and the attempt to develop markets and quasi-markets through which services should be provided, as documented in Ian Sanderson's chapter.

Needs assessment is of increasing concern to policy makers for a number of reasons. First, a number of new policy developments require by law, or strongly recommend, that needs assessments be carried out. My own chapter on community needs assessments makes this point in relation to recent urban regeneration initiatives; Martin Browne's chapter on community care draws attention to the requirements of the NHS and Community Care Act; Anne Foreman's chapter on health needs assessments makes reference to the guidelines relating to health needs assessments; and Mike Campbell's chapter on assessing training needs refers to recent policy statements in that context.

Second, in an environment of scarce resources, being able to demonstrate relatively high levels of need in your area can bring with it extra resources. Third, and relatedly, widening inequalities have resulted in a 'rediscovery' (again) of poverty and a concern to focus what resources are available on those who are in greatest need. However it is also important to note the point made in Ian Sanderson's chapter, that needs assessment, as a tool of targeting, can be used to hide the fact that fewer resources are available and that efforts are being concentrated primarily on a residual category of people deemed to have 'special needs'. As Bradshaw notes:

> In fact the word 'need' has become a smoke-screen to hide the true intention of policy, to camouflage policies which in their intention and effect have the purpose of increasing inequalities. If the word 'need' ever had any analytical purpose in the social sciences, it has been cynically adulterated in the last ten years or so.
>
> (Bradshaw 1994: 49)

Fourth, developments in the way in which public services are organized and managed, despite being born out of a concern to introduce elements of the market into public services, have resulted in an environment in which needs assessment is recognized as an essential input into the policy process, a point that is developed in Ian Sanderson's chapter and also in the case study chapters. Finally, at the political and ideological level, following the ascendancy of free market ideas over nearly two decades, we are beginning to see a revival of interest in and debates about social justice (see, for example, Coote 1992; Commission on Social Justice 1994) and what a welfare system for the future might look like. This is a far more conducive environment for discussion about needs and needs assessment.

The rationale for the present book is a concern that, while there is a considerable amount of work currently being undertaken in relation to needs assessment across a number of policy areas, there is considerable unevenness in the way that work is being carried out. Second, as is evident from the case study chapters, there are areas of common concern in relation to needs assessment in terms of theoretical and conceptual issues, methodologies and the way in which information on needs is used to inform or determine policy. These are not abstract concerns. What constitutes need, the methods used to assess need and the status that needs have in relation to services can determine whether or not, and at what level, services are provided to people and, consequently, whether or not need becomes disadvantage.

The structure and content of the book reflects these concerns. The papers in the first part of the book address theoretical, conceptual and methodological issues of relevance to needs assessment generally. In the remainder of this chapter I will present a brief overview of some recent theoretical debates around the concept of need and consider the implications of these debates for needs assessment methodologies and the policy process. In Chapter 2 Ian Sanderson discusses how need, rather than the market, can be used as the basis for the distribution of resources and the implications of this for public policy and public service management. In Chapter 3 David Porteous looks at a range of different approaches to assessing needs and the methods to which they give rise.

Part II consists of a series of case studies of areas in which needs assessment techniques are being used or are being developed. These chapters are not, of course, intended as an exhaustive account of needs assessment, rather they provide insight into a number of policy areas in which different approaches to needs assessment have been developed. Each of these chapters follows a broadly similar structure beginning with a discussion of the context within which needs assessment is occurring; identifying the theoretical and conceptual issues; discussing methods and methodologies; looking at impact or potential impact on service users and policy makers, and discussing problems and issues. In the concluding chapter I draw together the strands of the discussion by identifying common themes and issues.

In general, the case study chapters are concerned with the assessment of group or population needs although techniques for assessing the needs of individuals are also addressed where this is relevant to the methods of assessing population needs (see, for example, Martin Browne's chapter on assessing community care needs). The decision to focus on the macro level of needs assessment reflects our interest in the use of needs assessment as a tool to assist policy makers in decision making about resource allocation and the distribution of resources. Also at a methodological level the assessment of population needs gives rise to more difficult issues. As a result some important areas of policy where need might be considered to be a key issue are not included. The most obvious area is that of social security and welfare benefits. Here there is little room for manoeuvre at the local level since 'need' and the rules of eligibility that flow from this are, for the most part, defined centrally. As a result needs assessment takes place only at the level of individuals and their households and according to prescribed rules; local benefit offices merely administer a system the details of which are determined elsewhere. This is not the case with housing, training, community care or health where local authorities, health authorities and training and enterprise councils, in addition to providing certain services as laid down by statute, do have considerable discretion about what services should be provided, to whom and at what level. In these circumstances needs assessments, properly undertaken, are crucial to the development of appropriate and responsive services.

The needs debate

For much of the history of the welfare state the concept of needs has been taken pretty much for granted. A general, if implicit, consensus existed that meeting needs was what the welfare state was about, that those needs could be objectively identified, measured and used as a, if not the, criterion for gaining access to resources. Glennerster (1983: 43) sees this as a central element in the social administration tradition: 'Need was conceived of as an objective measurable quantity to be revealed by professional and social science enquiry and to provide the basis for the services to agree upon resource priorities.'

By the 1970s this view was coming under increasing attack from all sides of the political spectrum. The essence of the challenge related to the extent to which needs could be said to be absolute and objectively measurable. Orthodox economists especially, rejected the idea of objective human needs, arguing that needs are actually better described as subjective preferences or wants which individuals can choose to act on or not, in accordance with their own personal priorities, through activity in the market (see, for example, Williams 1974). In other words needs, conceptualized as subjective preferences, are not amenable to objective definition or measurement.

The New Right have taken this, essentially economic, argument one stage further into the political realm. Needs, it is claimed, are 'dangerous' (Doyal and Gough 1991: 10–11). To talk of objective need, defined by someone other than the individual themself, is to open the door to authoritarianism and infringements of individual liberty. In particular concern is expressed in relation to systems of taxation which force people to pay towards an end, or set of values, which they may not share. Needs, it is argued, presuppose value judgements:

> Even to describe social need ... we require some standards or criteria: needs do not just exist in the real world already labelled. To call a condition such as poverty, a social need implies an idea of what is not or ought not to be acceptable'.
>
> (Charles and Webb 1986: 11)

Underpinning this argument is the view that there can be no consensus about what would constitute a just distribution of resources or pattern of equality and inequality.

The meeting of 'needs' through publicly funded services is contrasted with, it is claimed, the morally neutral (because unintended) distribution of resources that occurs through the market as a result of people acting in accordance with their own self-determined preferences. Plant (1991, Ch. 5) among others, takes issue with this view of the operation of the market and argues that while the unequal outcomes that result from the operation of markets may be unintended, they are entirely foreseeable, and therefore not morally neutral at all.

Doyal and Gough (1991: 191–3) present a strong argument in favour of universal, objective, basic needs which they define as physical health and autonomy with a further 11 'intermediate needs' which, in all cultures, contribute to health and autonomy. These are: adequate nutritional food and clean water; adequate protective housing; a non-hazardous work environment; a non-hazardous physical environment; appropriate health care; security in childhood; significant primary relationships; physical security; economic security; appropriate education; and safe birth control and child bearing. Furthermore, they argue, that individuals alone may not be the best judges of what they need since they may lack appropriate knowledge or information about what is possible.

This issue of who can or should define need has also been addressed in a much quoted article by Bradshaw (1972). He argued that how needs are defined may reflect the values and perspectives of different groups. He presented a 'taxonomy of need' and argued that 'need' could be defined in four different ways. Normative needs are those defined in relation to an agreed standard which is determined by an expert or professional; those individuals or groups who fall short of this standard are identified as being in need. However it was recognized that this definition of need was likely to reflect, at least in part, the value judgements and interests of the professional groups involved. This would, in turn, differ from the felt needs of individuals, i.e. those needs that are identified by individuals themselves. Felt need is not the same as expressed need since felt needs may, for a variety of reasons, not be expressed (e.g. a felt need for housing may not generate an enquiry to the council if the individual believes that the council does not house people in their situation). Finally comparative need refers to the needs of a group of individuals relative to those of another group with similar characteristics. For Bradshaw 'real need' can be identified where these four perspectives coincide.

As a consequence the language of need is replaced by the language of priorities. The debate about needs can be summed up in the words of Plant as follows:

> Are there basic human needs and if there are what are the obligations of citizens and the state in respect of them? Can those needs be identified on an empirical basis and in what sense does the ascription of need presuppose some sort of expertise? How do we distinguish between needs and wants and what is the relation of each of these to interests?
>
> (Plant 1991: 185)

Plant, himself, has taken the debate forward by arguing that if in fact there are such things as basic needs, then these can and indeed should be used to underpin a set of enforceable social rights. He argues that social and economic inequalities arising from the operation of markets should not just be accepted. Rather 'citizenship confers a right to a central set of resources which can provide economic security, health and education – and this right exists irrespective of a person's standing in the market' (Plant 1992: 16).

This view has been challenged by those who argue that social and economic rights are not enforceable because they entail rights to resources which are necessarily scarce. However, Plant draws attention to the fact that civil and legal rights are also underpinned by resources (e.g. resources to provide policing, courts, etc.). Thus an argument against social and economic rights which has as a central plank the non-enforceability of rights requiring the expenditure of resources would also raise questions about the absolute nature of civil and political rights which are not, in fact, questioned. Allan Blake's discussion of needs in relation to legal services in Chapter 8 is instructive in this regard. Unlike most of the other policy areas discussed in the case study chapters, there is an absolute (formal) right to legal representation which the legal aid system is intended to transform into a substantive right for those unable to afford the cost of legal representation. However shortcomings of the system mean that this right is effectively undermined by lack of access to quality legal services in relation to certain areas of legal practice.

This absolute right to legal representation can be contrasted with the lack of rights in relation to community care. As Martin Browne shows in Chapter 4, fear of judicial review on the part of local authorities is affecting the way in which needs are recorded during care assessments to avoid specifying that an individual has a particular need which the authority cannot or will not provide for.

Assessing needs

If the idea of needs as the basis for the distribution of social goods is accepted then it is crucial that needs can be identified or assessed and that the methods used are appropriate. A number of issues are relevant here. First can needs be assessed effectively using secondary data, i.e. data that are collected for other purposes? Second, given that it is often difficult to collect data on needs themselves, we are often forced to use proxy indicators of need. How reliable and useful are these? Third, are professionals or 'experts' the best people to identify the needs of others? Might not their view be constrained by their own values and professional interests and their distance from those who are experiencing need? On the other hand focusing on individuals' and groups' own perspectives of need might also be limited by lack of knowledge about the possibilities of having their needs met, narrow horizons, powerlessness or a resigned acceptance of a state of affairs that they have simply learned to live with. Related to this is the issue of whether it is possible to identify needs in a group or an individual in a way that is not stigmatizing or disempowering to that individual or group. Finally, while it is undoubtedly important for certain purposes to be able to quantify needs, is there nevertheless a role for qualitative research methods which allow needs to be not only counted but also understood?

The range of methods used in relation to needs assessment is reviewed by David Porteous in Chapter 3. In addition the case study chapters also examine issues and problems associated with particular approaches to, and techniques for, needs assessment that are especially relevant to those policy areas.

From needs to policy

Information about needs, if it is to be more than a rallying call for action to be taken, must be capable of being used effectively in the determination of policy, i.e. what services should be provided, or action taken, to whom, at what level, how and by whom should such services be delivered. Information on needs could be used at a number of different points in the policy process. It might be used strategically to determine the allocation of resources between services or policy areas, between geographical areas or population groups. It might be used to determine service priorities. It might be used to inform decision making about the types of services to be provided and in what way, to ensure that services are developed that not only respond to people's needs but do so in a way that is acceptable to them. And it might be used in monitoring and evaluation by providing a means of assessing progress made.

However a number of issues are relevant here that will be picked up again in the case study chapters and also in the conclusion. First to what extent can or should needs be used as the criterion for gaining access to resources? Second if this is the case then should there not be clear guidelines on how to assess needs in order to ensure that like needs receive like treatment? At the moment this is certainly not the case, as Martin Browne and Murray Hawtin demonstrate in their respective chapters on community care and housing. If we take community care as an example, local authorities have the responsibility for assessing both individual and collective needs without any statement or definition of need being provided centrally. And, since need alone is not a sufficient condition for resources or services being provided, local authorities also have the responsibility for drawing up eligibility criteria for community care services. The result is that individuals living in different localities but having the same needs will not receive the same level of community care services. Or individuals living in the same locality but whose needs are assessed by different people may not receive the same assessment and therefore services. This raises serious questions about the validity of needs assessment techniques. Third, as I have argued elsewhere (Percy-Smith 1992), assessing or identifying needs does not, in an environment of scarce resources, answer in a technocratic manner the question of who should get what. That question should be a matter for open, political debate. However, systematically collected, reliable information about the needs of different sections of the population, together with a clear commitment to a vision of social justice that is informed by the idea that needs ought to be met, gives a better basis for that debate and the process of decision making than the inadequate and partial information that is available now.

This book is intended to be of practical assistance to those practitioners and policy makers who are grappling with the difficult task of undertaking needs assessment in an environment in which there is little shared understanding of what constitutes social need or guidance on how to undertake needs assessment. It is also intended as a practical contribution to the ongoing theoretical and political debate about need by drawing attention to some of the issues that arise when attempts are made to operationalize the concept of need through needs assessments.

References

Bradshaw, J. (1972) The concept of social need, *New Society*, 30 March: 640–3.

Bradshaw, J. (1994) The conceptualization and measurement of need. A social policy perspective. In J. Popay and G. Williams (eds) *Researching People's Health*. London: Routledge.

Charles, S.T. and Webb, A.L. (1986) *The Economic Approach to Social Policy*. Brighton: Wheatsheaf Books.

Commission on Social Justice (1994) *Social Justice: Strategies for National Renewal. The Report of the Commission*. London: Vintage.

Coote, A. (ed.) (1992) *The Welfare of Citizens. Developing New Social Rights*. London: IPPR/Rivers Oram Press.

Doyal, L. and Gough, I. (1991) *A Theory of Human Need*. London: Macmillan.

Glennerster, H. (1983) *Planning for Priority Groups*. Oxford: Martin Robertson.

Percy-Smith, J. (1992) Auditing social needs, *Policy and Politics*, 20 (1): 29–34.

Plant, R. (1991) *Modern Political Thought*. Oxford: Blackwell.

Plant, R. (1992) Citizenship, rights and welfare. In A. Coote (ed.) *The Welfare of Citizens. Developing New Social Rights*. London: IPPR/Rivers Oram Press.

Williams, A. (1974) 'Need' as a demand concept. In A.J. Culyer (ed.) *Economic Policies and Social Goals*. Oxford: Martin Robertson.

IAN SANDERSON

NEEDS AND PUBLIC SERVICES

Introduction

Need is a controversial concept. It is the subject of dispute in debates about how resources should be allocated in the provision of public services; how governments should decide between competing claims on the welfare state. However, the controversy goes deeper than this, ultimately reflecting deep-seated disputes about the desirable scale and scope of public welfare services and, underpinning such disputes, conflicts of viewpoint on the nature of human society. Discussion of need is inherently normative; as Charles and Webb (1986: 11) state: 'To call a condition, such as poverty, a social need implies an idea of what is not or ought not to be acceptable.' This makes need a contested notion. Thus, on the one hand, those who regard the allocation of welfare and the performance of social institutions as a 'technical' matter subject to value-free enquiry and empirical determination will reject the validity of need. On the other hand, the existence of conflicting interests and values in society renders slight the prospect of consensus around both the validity of the term and the definition of particular social needs.

Underpinning the controversy, then, are conflicting perspectives on the welfare state: on its desirable size, scope and role; on the role of the state in providing welfare services; on the principles by which welfare should be distributed; and on the desirable ends of social organization (Williams 1989). Put simply, such perspectives are distinguished in terms of the degree of support for a collective commitment, via the state, for welfare provision on the basis of need as opposed to support for a market-based society which maximizes the scope of individual choice and relegates the state to a minimal 'safety net' role (Williams 1989: 18–22). The primary basis for conflict lies in assumptions about the role of the individual in achieving social change. Thus advocates of the free market, or 'anti-collectivists', see individual action and initiative driven by self-interest as the basis for a society which combines economic efficiency and personal liberty. On the other hand, advocates of collective action emphasize the role of social structures and institutions in shaping and constraining individuals' circumstances, perceptions and behaviour and the consequent need for public policy to promote equal opportunity for all (Coote 1992).

Those 'ranged passionately on either side of this conceptual divide' (Minford 1987: 70) take very different positions in relation to the concept of need. To anti-collectivists it is the mantra of collectivism, representing the intrusion, or even tyranny, of the state, interfering with, and overriding, individual freedom of choice at the cost of inefficiency and dependency. To *laissez-faire* economists it is an essentially vacuous concept; only individuals' demands backed by a willingness and ability to pay are seen as having relevance in discussions about resource allocation:

> need can only be a useful concept if it is equated to a demand by governments or individuals for goods and services. So long as prices and quantities are omitted from estimations of 'need', the concept can have neither theoretical nor empirical value, and it properly belongs not to the social sciences but to the vocabulary of political rhetoric.
>
> (Nevin quoted in Sinfield 1980: 180–1)

On the other hand, to collectivists need provides the essential basis for decisions on the provision of welfare services. Because markets are prone to various forms of 'failure' and result in inequalities in outcomes, government action is required to promote efficiency and equity. Elected politicians and professionals employed by the state must have a role in assessing the needs of individuals and communities in order to ensure socially 'optimal' outcomes.

Adopting a stance in this debate is not primarily an empirical matter; it is much more about values, in particular the relative valuation of individualist and egalitarian ends. The policies of Conservative governments since 1979 have embodied the anti-collectivist celebration of individualism but, as Johnson (1990: 3) argues, 'public support for the ideas underpinning the welfare state is as strong as it has ever been'. Nevertheless, there is a tension which needs to be addressed:

> The social contract which legitimises the welfare state is in question. Do we still want the state to provide for us? How much are we prepared to pay to meet the needs of others? Will the rich ever again be willing to redistribute wealth to the poor? Where should the state's duty towards us start and our own responsibility for ourselves and for our families stop?
>
> (Phillips 1995)

At the centre of this debate the key issues concern the extent to which, and the circumstances in which, individual choice and responsibility are overridden by collective action by government, the grounds for entitlement to welfare services and the scale and source of resources to finance such services. In this chapter we consider arguments around these issues. In the next section we review very briefly the traditional social administration perspective on needs and social policy. This is followed by a discussion of the New Right perspective which has dominated government policy since 1979. We then elaborate a critique of this perspective on both 'technical' and 'normative' grounds arguing that there is a case on the grounds of both allocative efficiency and distributive justice for collective action to address needs. We argue that this case is strengthened by evidence of the impact of New Right policies implemented since 1979. An approach to 'needs-driven' public policy is presented which relates needs to 'desired social outcomes' and argues for the empowerment of citizens through political strategies to promote 'voice'. In conclusion, we emphasize that in advocating collective action to meet needs and promote social justice we are engaging in an inherently political debate about social ends and desirable forms of economic, social and political organization.

The social administration tradition

The traditional social administration perspective holds that the purpose of public social services is to meet need. As Bradshaw (1972: 640) argued: 'The concept of social need is inherent in the idea of social service. The history of the social services is the history of the recognition of social needs and the organisation of society to meet them.' From this perspective, need was conceived of as an objective measurable quantity to be revealed by professional and social science enquiry, which provided the basis for agreement about resource priorities (Glennerster 1983: 43). It is underpinned by the assumption of consensus deriving either from the idea of 'objective necessity' or from the assumed existence of 'shared values born of common humanity' (Hill and Bramley 1986: 58). Need provides the basis for rationing, for 'the prioritisation of competing claims in the face of restricted resources' (Taylor-Gooby and Dale 1981: 23). Moreover, needs are essentially defined from the perspective of the state in terms of the services which are available, in a context dominated by professional and bureaucratic interests (Taylor-Gooby and Dale 1981; Glennerster 1983: 44–5).

This perspective dominated the post-World War II consensus on the welfare state but has come under criticism from both Left and Right. From the Left there is criticism of the consensual assumptions underlying the notion of objective need and a focus on the implications of conflicting values and interests. Needs are seen as socially created; different groups will have competing claims which should be the subject of open political debate. Moreover, if needs are defined from state professionals' viewpoints as the basis for rationing available welfare services, the possibility that our form of economy and society cannot satisfy needs adequately is excluded from debate (Taylor-Gooby and Dale 1981; Walker 1984).

Some degree of consensus has emerged between Left and Right about the extent to which the state 'has become overly bureaucratic, remote from the needs of many of the people it is meant to address, and ... has become the servant of powerfully entrenched producer interests rather than the users of these services' (Hambleton and Hoggett 1993: 104). However, the reform strategies of Left and Right are radically different. It is the thinking of the 'New Right' which has dominated government policies since 1979 and we now discuss briefly the implications of such thinking for the provision of welfare services.

The New Right perspective

The ideas of the New Right are fundamentally anti-collectivist, based upon the economic liberal belief that freedom of the individual is the ultimate goal in judging social arrangements. Individual action and initiative are seen as the primary forces behind social change and should be protected; the notion that individual behaviour is constrained or determined by forces outside their control is rejected as undermining the notion of individual responsibility (Plant *et al.* 1980: 175–7; Minford 1987: 70). Individual freedom is seen as best promoted in market economies in which a decentralized exchange system, conducted within a general system of law, operates in a self-regulating fashion to achieve efficient allocation of resources (Barry 1987).

From this perspective there is a fundamental hostility towards 'interference' by the state which undermines individual freedom of choice. The welfare state is criticized on three grounds (Williams 1989: 25–6). First, the state is seen as 'the primary force of coercion threatening individual liberty' (King 1987: 36) through the burden of taxation necessary to finance welfare services; through planning and legal controls which inhibit private enterprise; and through the paternalism and authoritarianism of monopoly public service providers in deciding how needs for welfare should be met. Second, these monopoly characteristics are also seen as leading to inefficiency and waste due to lack of competition, exacerbated by escalating public demand for services and the behaviour of self-interested professionals and bureaucrats. Finally, the welfare state is seen as morally disruptive because it undermines individual initiative and self-reliance; thus, according to Ranade and Haywood (1989:21), it 'induces dependency and reduces incentives to work, individual and family responsibility, initiative and enterprise'.

The critique of the inherent inefficiency of state bureaucracies has been informed by 'public choice' theory which sees the state not as serving to maximize society's welfare but rather as comprising self-interested actors pursuing their own political advantage (King 1987: 92–100; Self 1993: 3–9). It is argued, on the one hand, that voters will seek to maximize their individual welfare by voting for parties which offer most in terms of public goods and services without being immediately aware of the costs or revenue sources of government programmes. On the other hand, in order to achieve election politicians will tend to offer more, causing the demands placed upon government to exceed resources, resulting in government overload and possible failure. Large, effectively organized interest groups also encourage the growth of government programmes. Moreover, as indicated above, bureaucrats and professionals in government are assumed to maximize their own advantage, in terms of income, status and power, by pushing for increased budgets and, because of their monopoly position, they are able to exaggerate costs of provision. The result is an oversupply of welfare services relative to citizens' actual preferences. In effect, the interests of citizens who need and use public services are subordinated to the interests of 'producers' (Mishra 1984: 28–42; King 1987: 100–4; Self 1993: 57–8).

Public choice theory complements free market economic theory to produce a powerful critique of the state. Within the New Right position, then, a market society is to be preferred on the grounds of both efficiency in the use of resources and moral superiority. The notion that markets produce social injustice is rejected along with the attendant claim that the assessment of needs can provide a basis for conferring on citizens rights to welfare services in order to achieve social justice. Thus it is argued that in the absence of clear rules and principles about a 'just' distribution of resources, a regime of social justice based upon needs and rights simply serves to entrench at the heart of the state a wholly undesirable degree of professional and bureaucratic power (Plant 1992: 19–20).

Clearly the ideas of the New Right have had a major influence on the policies and programmes of Conservative governments since 1979 which have involved extensive privatization and 'marketization'. The private sector has been encouraged to provide alternative, privately based welfare; parts of state welfare services have been contracted out to the private sector; and private market principles have been increasingly applied within state welfare services. The intention is to make services more efficient and more accountable and responsive to consumers who are now better able to exercise choice. A further element in the erosion of the role of the state has been the encouragement of the family to exercise greater responsibility for the care of dependent children and elderly people (Williams 1989: 26). However, the New Right position can be criticized on a number of grounds which we now discuss.

The challenge to the New Right

The challenge to the New Right position addresses both economic and political aspects. The critique of economic liberalism comprises 'technical' and 'normative' components. The 'technical' component addresses the proposition that market economies generate optimality in the allocation of resources while the 'normative' component is pursued on the moral or ethical level to challenge the justification of inequality in market societies with reference to the promotion of individual freedom and initiative. The concept of 'market failure' is commonly applied in the argument that markets will habitually fail to produce outcomes which are either 'technically efficient' in the sense that goods and services are produced at lowest possible cost, or 'socially efficient' in the sense that the distribution of resources is optimal in terms of satisfying individual preferences (i.e. Pareto optimal).[1] There are a number of reasons why markets 'fail' and we will discuss these briefly (Knapp 1984; LeGrand and Robinson 1984; Charles and Webb 1986; Levacic 1987; Wistow *et al.* 1994).

First, consumers rarely have perfect knowledge of the goods and services on offer, particularly in the case of complex services such as health where a high degree of professionalization may compound the problem. Second, monopoly power commonly accrues to producers by virtue of economies of scale for highly specialized services and the existence of 'natural' spatial monopolies which restrict choice in small areas (e.g. schools and hospitals). In the context of social care Wistow *et al.* (1994: 100–5) consider a range of sources of 'structural imperfections' in the market, arguing that 'few social care markets will contain enough actual or potential purchasers or providers to prevent these structural imperfections arising' (Wistow *et al.* 1994: 100). Thus they argue that there are too few suppliers with the capacity to provide effective supply-side competition; that there are significant barriers to entry into the market (e.g. capital and resource constraints) which raise questions about its 'contestability'; and that there may be resistance, particularly in the voluntary sector, to contractual arrangements (Wistow *et al.* 1994). If there are problems of imperfect consumer knowledge and structural imperfections in competition, the technical efficiency of market outcomes will be impaired.

However, the social efficiency of the market is also undermined by the third and most serious cause of market failure which derives from the existence of 'externalities'. These are side-effects of either production or consumption which are not taken into account in resource allocation or pricing decisions. External costs arise when disbenefits are borne by people other than the producers or consumers of a good or service (e.g. traffic congestion, pollution) whereas external benefits arise when there are collective benefits (e.g. education and training, immunization). Individual decision making in the market will result in overproduction/consumption where there are external costs and underproduction/consumption where there are external benefits, relative to a socially optimal outcome. A special type of externality occurs in the case of 'public goods' which display characteristics of 'non-rivalness' (i.e. one person's consumption does not reduce the supply for others) and 'non-excludability' (i.e. nobody can be excluded from enjoying the benefits). Examples of public goods include defence, street lighting and fire services. Market provision of such goods and services would create problems of 'free riders' because individuals could refuse to bear the cost while still enjoying the benefits.

The existence of market failures provides a case for collective mechanisms which override individual decision making in the market and, indeed, this is acknowledged by advocates of market societies. Thus Barry (1987: 170) argues that: 'Apart from a minority of extremists (called "anarcho-capitalists") all classical liberal market economists accept that certain goods and services have to be supplied by the state.' A more radical critique maintains that such an acceptance, justified with reference to the concept of externalities serves to legitimize the market system by defining a restricted scope for the state. Thus Walker (1984: 49–56) argues that by definition the concept of externality defines adverse consequences of the market as outside the scope of the normal operation of the economy. As such, they are marginalized as the concern of social policy and therefore seen as treatable by the state and not as implying fundamental flaws in the market system which require a change in economic relations. Walker maintains that the Pareto optimality criterion of social efficiency plays a central role in legitimizing the market system by justifying limited state action:

> It is anti-collectivist because it assumes that the state will not intervene unless the market fails and therefore that the role of the state should,

ideally, be confined to dealing with 'externalities'. It is individualistic, assuming both that the market is politically neutral and that the distribution of original income is fair.

(Walker 1984: 58)

This criticism raises the issue of distributive justice. If there are grounds for questioning the fairness of this 'distribution of original income' then more radical collective action would be justified which would begin to change fundamentally the basis upon which wealth and resources are distributed in society. Again, market economists will acknowledge the case for limited state action to address equity issues through, for example, subsidies and benefits for those in 'real need'. However, New Right thinking does not accept that market outcomes are fundamentally unjust. Thus it is argued that so long as such outcomes are the *unintended* consequences of individual acts of free exchange, then no injustice is incurred no matter how unequal the distribution of income and wealth (Plant 1992: 19–20). This position can be criticized on the grounds that inequality is a *foreseeable* (if not intended) consequence of the operation of markets and hence can be subjected to a moral critique with reference to concepts of social justice which would justify more radical state action (Plant 1992: 24–5).

Underpinning the New Right position, then, is the basic assumption of the primacy of individual choice, freedom and liberty and the prescriptions of technical and social efficiency of the market are derived under 'the mask of positive, value-free scientific enquiry' (Charles and Webb 1986: 41). In fact, there is no neutrality and value-freedom here; the normative position adopted has no inherent superiority to one which advocates principles of social justice based upon collective egalitarian notions. The choice should be a matter of political debate rather than the result of an inherently biased valuation of market versus state forms of provision:

[T]here is a tendency among critics of state provision to compare the state with all its known and admitted defects of bureaucracy and centralisation with the *theoretical* model of the perfect market. The defects of the latter are minimised and seen to be remedial, while those of the former are maximised and are seen to be inherent and unchanging

(Charles and Webb 1986: 69)

This brings us to the political dimension of the critique. We have seen that New Right thinking accommodates some government action to address the (minimized) failures of the market; yet the scope of such action is further circumscribed by the emphasis on 'government failure'. Culyer (1980: 50) summarizes the argument as follows:

[I]f the market 'fails' then it must contain within itself its own self-correcting procedures. To jump from the observation of market failure to the assertion that the government can 'do things better' is, however, a hopeless *non sequitur* . . . collective action can also 'fail'.

The 'government failure' thesis is criticized by Mishra (1984) on a number of grounds. He argues that it is exaggerated and based upon selective evidence;

in reality the growth of the welfare state cannot be explained solely by reference to 'capture' by vested interests. Moreover, echoing the point made above, it represents a biased view of the state, criticizing 'big government' but supporting big business, failing to acknowledge the implications of the political process. Indeed, he argues that it is underpinned by an inadequate conception of the role of democracy and politics, in turn premised, as referred to earlier, on the values of individualism and the rejection of the notion of collective interest as the foundation for criticizing market outcomes as 'socially unjust' (Mishra 1984: 54–61).

This latter theme is emphasized by Self (1993) who argues that the rejection of the notion of collective interest legitimizes selfish individual behaviour by making it appear rational and universal, hence acceptable. Moreover, the 'reduction' of political liberty to market freedom creates the danger of the former being suppressed in the promotion of the latter due to the failure to acknowledge that the market operates within 'political rules' created by the state and that '[w]hatever the state does or does not do will have a considerable effect upon the distribution of . . . resources and of consequent individual opportunities to exercise liberty' (Self 1993: 255). By abstracting the operation of the market from politics, its outcomes are legitimized with reference to 'the necessary logic of a superior system':

> Consequently, individuals' claims to moral consideration through the political process became illegitimate or at best somewhat peripheral, depending upon the personal altruistic tastes which some citizens happen to possess. Equally irrelevant is the idea that some forms of human welfare derive from the quality of relationships between individuals, not from their private wants. Such relationships may be sought through private associations or clubs, but they are assumed to have little place in politics.
>
> (Self 1993: 255)

For the New Right, then, the answer to 'big government' is 'minimal government' and we have referred to policies of privatization and marketization, compulsory competitive tendering, the introduction of quasi-markets and the promotion of managerialist strategies to improve efficiency and cost-effectiveness. An important theme in such policies is the empowerment of consumers – the attempt to introduce the key desideratum of the framework of market economics, namely individual choice. Thus, accountability to the consumer is seen as promoted through the power of 'exit', the ability of consumers to choose to take their business elsewhere: 'Whenever the client can exercise a choice, the most effective form of redress is the right of exit: the decision not to accept the service provided and to go somewhere else' (HMSO 1991: 50).

In the context of public services, however, the exit strategy for empowerment is subject to serious criticism on the grounds of the absence of the fundamental prerequisites for free individual choice. We have already covered some of the main problems above in our discussion of 'market failures' – structural imperfections in competition, lack of information and the existence of 'externalities' which justify collective action. There are many public services which are public precisely because the economic conditions for effective exit strategies are not present. Moreover, the argument cannot be confined to economic grounds, abstracted from broader political considerations. Thus the relationship between the user/client of many public services and the service provider cannot be reduced to one of economic exchange. Rather, there is necessarily a power relationship whereby individual choice is overridden by collective mandate to achieve social control (e.g. police, prisons), regulation (e.g. social work, environmental health, planning) or due to the need to ration resources (e.g. housing waiting lists). Achieving accountability in such circumstances requires attention to forms of political representation rather than to economic mechanisms (Hambleton and Hoggett 1993).

Consequently, the exit model can be seen as reinforcing the legitimation of market society; it appears (falsely) to offer a route to empowering those who have to rely on the (minimal) public services which are justified by acknowledged 'market failures' thus underpinning the assumption of sovereign individuals able to exercise effective choice in markets. In cases where it is acknowledged that the power of exit is limited, the answer is to provide charters conferring certain rights on consumers who are dissatisfied with the service they receive – the government's *Citizen's Charter* emphasizes the right to complain and receive effective 'redress' (HMSO 1991). However, again these limited rights embody an impoverished notion of politics and do not permit fundamental criticism of broader political choices and policies; in effect they help to legitimize the social and economic relations of the market society. Thus Donnison (1994: 23) criticizes the 'charter approach' in the following terms:

> It offers customer's rights for individuals dissatisfied with the service they receive – because their train was late or their leaking roof took weeks to repair, for example. Useful though those are, they are not the citizen's rights which enable people to question the way in which their society is evolving – to ask for a different kind of transport system, for more public housing or for housing allocated to different kinds of people, for example.

A final aspect of the legitimatory role of New Right thinking relates back to the notions of 'market failure' and 'externalities'. We referred earlier to Walker's (1984) argument that acknowledged adverse effects of the market system are minimized and marginalized through the concept of externalities which defines them as outside the scope of economic solutions and capable of amelioration through social policy. Thus the fundamental economic relations of market society are protected from challenge; the impression is given that 'real needs' arising from adverse effects of the market are being met. Clapham and Smith (1990) develop this position, arguing in the housing context that the concept of 'special need' plays an important role in New Right thinking in legitimizing the limited role of the state in market society. Thus if government action is justified in relation to 'special' (or 'abnormal') need, this implies that 'normal' needs can be met through the market. Special needs can then be identified with groups 'deserving' of state action with two implications:

> First, it publicises the caring face of market liberalism by making limited provision for those who, it is assumed, could not otherwise participate in

the fruits of popular capitalism. This helps legitimise neo-liberalism's strategy of 'moderate' inequality in a competitive economy.

Secondly, this 'special needs' approach constructs the wider problem of housing disadvantage as something that is discrete (empirically limited in its extent and duration), and that is a moral rather than structural issue which can be solved through technical or administrative (rather than political) change.

(Clapham and Smith 1990: 199)

This critique of the New Right position provides the basis for advocating collective action to achieve social outcomes radically different from those achieved through the market system. This is justified on the grounds of both allocative efficiency (to 'correct' market failures) and distributive justice, rejecting the notion of Paretian social efficiency and addressing explicitly the social justice of the prevailing distribution of income and wealth. It is also justified by rejecting the value judgements built into the model of the free market economy (on the grounds that these are politically negotiable and not 'inherently superior') and the individualistic framework of explanation. In particular, it is argued that the behaviour of individuals can be understood only in the context of their economic, social and cultural circumstances and that values relating to the development of non-exchange relationships and to egalitarian notions of social justice are important. As Charles and Webb (1986: 71) argue:

If the quality of social relationships is seen to be of major importance . . . there is good reason to place its achievement on a par with efficiency . . . If the market is found to reduce trust, inhibit altruistic behaviour and limit social justice, the issue ought not to be whether to take a few areas of 'social' provision out of the market, but which areas of social life to allow the market to handle.

Indeed, this case can be seen as strengthened by the evidence of the impact of New Right policies implemented by Conservative governments since 1979 in relation to the above criteria of trust, altruistic behaviour and social justice. In the next section we consider very briefly some of this evidence.

The impact of New Right policies

Social injustice is real. It hurts. And in Britain it is growing worse . . . Growing numbers of people are being excluded by poverty from the mainstream of Western societies . . . That is because their economies are becoming increasingly unequal.

(Donnison 1994: 1, 4)

There is considerable evidence of increasing inequality in Britain due to the implementation of policies inspired by New Right thinking. This is extensively documented in an inquiry by the Joseph Rowntree Foundation (Hills 1995). Self (1993: 212) argues that the 'revival of Victorian *laissez-faire* thinking has persuaded governments to cut welfare services and public investment, to accept high levels of unemployment as a necessary evil, and to put downward pressure on wages'. He maintains that the growth of unemployment was exacerbated by the removal of industrial subsidies and the rundown of public investment in the depressed industrial regions (Self 1993: 90). Various measures have been aimed at reducing the wages of the lower paid (e.g. curtailment of employment rights, abolition of wage councils, weakening of trade unions) while a *laissez-faire* approach has been adopted in relation to the more highly paid (Johnson 1990: 198–9). To quote Donnison (1994: 10) again:

> Working conditions, security of employment and fringe benefits for those in the lower reaches of the labour market have been eroded . . .
>
> Meanwhile, at the top, greed has been unbridled: senior managers, who have already been given huge reductions in tax, award themselves vast increases in pay, almost without regard to the success of their (frequently ailing) enterprises.

Moreover, changes in taxation and state benefits have also contributed to growing inequality. Changes to income tax, VAT and national insurance contributions have made the tax system less progressive (Johnson 1990: 201; Hills 1995: 56–61). The impact of changes in state benefits is summarized by Williams (1989: 169):

> As well as unemployment and low pay, the declining value of state benefits, of pensions, supplementary benefits . . . income support, child benefits, widow's benefits and the losses of entitlement in housing benefit, free school meals, maternity grant, disablement allowance, young people's allowances, all contribute to the creation of more and more people living on the poverty line.

Williams (1989: 171–2) further argues that policies of privatization, the introduction of market principles within state welfare, contracting out and increased use of charges have affected women and black people particularly harshly, reinforcing the gender and race dimensions of inequality (see also Johnson 1990: 210–15). Changes in particular public services have had a significant impact on inequality. For example, the reduction in the supply of public housing, due to council house sales and restriction of local authority new building, combined with the increase in rents due to the restriction on rent subsidies, have contributed to a substantial increase in homelessness and in the housing costs of the poor (Johnson 1990). As regards reforms to health services, a recent survey of public health directors found that more than half believed the principle of equality of access to care had been weakened by the reforms (Marks 1995).

The evidence of the impact of New Right policies supports the case of those who argue that egalitarian notions of social justice are as legitimate as notions of efficiency and individual freedom as values to be achieved by economic and social organization and who reject the implicit justification of 'natural inequality' in the market framework. The balance and trade-off between these values should be a matter of explicit political debate and negotiation but the more that the quality of social relationships and the achievement of social justice are valued, the greater will be the case for collective action to meet 'social needs' which will complement, and to some extent override, individual action in the market to satisfy wants.

A key issue from this perspective, then, is how needs-driven collective action can be made to be effective and to operate in the interests of the majority of citizens who have no special privilege in terms of wealth and power, and especially in the interests of the poor and disadvantaged whose needs must be addressed effectively in order that the desired degree of social justice can be achieved. In addressing this issue we must have regard to the force of criticism of the 'capture' of state bureaucracies by powerfully entrenched producer interests who produce 'expert' definitions of needs influenced by particular values, knowledge and ideologies and by the services which are perceived as appropriate or actually capable of being provided given resource constraints. Under these circumstances it is evident that much state welfare provision has not been directed at the needs of the poor and disadvantaged (LeGrand 1982). In the next section we consider some issues around the development of needs-driven public services.

Towards needs-based public services?

The discussion of appropriate forms of collective action to address needs requires issues to be addressed on two levels. On the first level consideration needs to be given to strategies for 'correcting' the operation of the market in order to achieve desired outcomes – to promote patterns of income distribution, consumption and resource allocation which are consistent with notions of social justice. This involves intervention to modify patterns of individual choices of goods and services through regulation, redistribution (e.g. via subsidies) or replacement of market mechanisms by state provision (Charles and Webb 1986: 86–7).

On the second level the focus is on strategies to ensure that providers of goods and services are responsive to the needs of consumers or citizens and that there is no undue domination by producer interests. This may involve regulation of markets to ensure effective competition between private producers, but in relation to public provision we indicated above the limitations of 'exit' strategies based upon the premise of individual choice. In order to provide effective accountability of public services to citizens there is a need to increase their 'voice' – to give them the power to influence decision making and to call service providers to account if they have grievances. This implies improved forms of democratic participation in approaches to needs assessment and satisfaction (Coote 1993; Hambleton and Hoggett 1993).

Underpinning these considerations, of course, is the issue of defining the concept of 'need'. This is the subject of another chapter but a brief discussion is required here. Setting aside the objections of economic liberals, the definition of need is still a matter of considerable controversy and dispute because it is used in a variety of ways and for a variety of purposes in the complex public policy process (Charles and Webb 1986: 13). Thus need may be expressed in terms of addressing social problems, producing certain policy outputs or achieving outcomes. Statements of need may be used as a means of moral or political persuasion, as diagnoses of social problems, as policy statements, or to define decisions to allocate resources (Charles and Webb 1986: 13–16).

In developing a model for effective public service provision, it is the relationship of the concept of need to social problems and outcomes which is of most interest. This point is underlined by Culyer (1980) who argues that need implies the accomplishment of a desired end-state and that this raises two issues for public policy: first, the definition of 'desired outcomes'; and second, the assessment of the effectiveness of various means to the achievement of these outcomes. This has important implications for public policy in terms of the processes used to arrive at judgements as to 'desired outcomes' and priorities between them, and the assessment of the impact of social policies in relation to these outcomes (Culyer 1980: 69–70, 192–4).

From this perspective, needs-based public policy must be focused on outcomes. The fundamental purpose of social policy is to achieve effectively (and efficiently) those outcomes which are socially-perceived as the most valued in relation to the diagnosis of social problems and the valuation of social ends. The analysis of social problems and the prioritization of desired outcomes must accommodate the perspectives and interests of the full range of relevant 'stakeholders' whose views should also count in decisions on appropriate policies and allocations of resources. However, fundamental to such decisions will be the assessment of effectiveness in achieving the desired outcomes which must address first, the extent to which the outcomes are achievable at all within the scope of available policy instruments and second, the relative effectiveness of alternative available means. Of course, this raises the issue of the scope for radical change in economic and social policies which might be necessary to achieve the desired outcomes. Finally, a crucial component in such a policy process must be the evaluation of adopted policies and courses of action in terms of the extent to which they achieve in practice the intended outcomes (need satisfaction) in order to learn lessons and improve the capacity of the policy process to recognize and prioritize needs and to address and meet them effectively.

A number of implications follow from the adoption of such a model. From this perspective, quality in the public service context must be defined in terms of the extent to which needs as desired outcomes are met. Thus quality cannot simply be a matter of meeting defined service standards or achieving 'customer satisfaction' but rather must involve questions about the appropriateness of policies and the adequacy of resources in relation to defined needs. The key concept in evaluation, therefore, is effectiveness. From this point of view, the tendency of public service organizations to focus on economy and efficiency measures can be criticized as failing to address the definition of performance that really matters (Pollitt and Harrison 1992) and as serving to protect underlying policies and resource allocation decisions from scrutiny.

A model of public service provision truly focused on effectiveness in relation to need presents two key challenges to the existing structure and organization of public services. First, the fragmentation of responsibility for public services, which is increasing with the growth of quangos at the expense of elected government (Weir and Hall 1994), militates against the definition of needs which require a broad ranging policy response. Given the tendency for organizations to define needs in terms of the services which they provide, such fragmentation will tend to result in the neglect of the more severe social problems such as poverty on the grounds that no one organization has the powers and resources to tackle them. Consequently, the development of effective strategies to address such problems can be seen as requiring a reversal of the trend towards fragmentation. This might involve, for example, the extension of the powers, responsibilities and resources of elected local authorities and the strengthening of interagency collaboration and coordination.

Second, if there is to be a genuine focus on effectiveness in relation to need, then the public policy process must be opened up and democratized. The established interests within public service organizations which restrict the definition of performance to protect the existing power structure must be challenged and made accountable to all the relevant stakeholders. The 'customers' of services are important stakeholders who need to be given a voice in the public policy process but the limitations of the consumerist model discussed earlier mean that there are dangers in the notion of 'customer orientation' in public services (Pollitt 1988). It is important that all relevant interests are involved including those who may be unable to gain access to the services they need and those representing groups and communities as a whole where there is a 'collective interest' which may conflict with individual consumer interests (for example, arising out of 'externalities').

These two challenges imply a pluralist approach to needs assessment and policy formulation which can produce democratically negotiated definitions of the desired outcomes from public policies, of priorities for need satisfaction consistent with the promotion of social justice, and of policies and allocation of resources. It implies, in effect, a shift of power towards those who are disadvantaged in a market society and towards 'collective interests'. It implies a focus on the promotion of 'citizenship' whereby people are empowered to become fully involved in the processes of government. This raises the issue of the means by which citizens might be empowered in relation to the provision of welfare services to achieve social justice. We can define two possible strategies: the first entails empowerment through rights; the second empowerment through voice. We now discuss them briefly in turn.

Citizen empowerment through rights

Coote (1992: 1) argues that 'the idea of enforceable social rights offers a new way of empowering citizens, different from the traditional models of empowerment favoured by the Right (market choices) and by the Left (democratic accountability)'. The notion of social rights implies a valid conception of social justice. We referred earlier to the New Right proposition that the concept of social justice has no moral purchase because the outcomes of markets are not intentional and it is not possible to develop through political negotiation a conception of a fair allocation of resources. Advocates of social rights reject this position and argue that it is possible to formulate a moral critique of markets in terms of social justice because the consequences of markets are entirely foreseeable (Plant 1992).

From this perspective, enforceable social rights are seen as a means to achieving social justice and as a way of empowering citizens in relation to public services in response to the idea that 'there is a social dimension to citizenship' (Plant 1992: 27). This entails extending the political rights of citizenship beyond the market place, as Coote (1992: 4) argues:

> Citizenship entails being able to participate in society, to enjoy its fruits and to fulfil one's own potential, and it follows that each individual citizen must be equally able (or 'empowered') to do so. This suggests two things: first, that all individuals must have equal access to education, health care and other services necessary to give them an equal chance in life. Second, no-one should be subject to unfair discrimination.

The notion of equalizing the life chances of all represents a social outcome, indicating the close relationship between rights and needs. Thus the right to a minimum standard of welfare can be seen as related to the absolute concept of need. Charles and Webb (1986: 71) put the case thus: 'Certain needs are so fundamental, it may be argued, that they should be treated as a social right and society should accept a duty to provide them to all citizens.'

This argument is developed by Plant *et al.* (1980: 58–96) who consider three possible moral bases for welfare – justice, rights and needs – and conclude that a coherent treatment of the first two concepts is contingent upon the notion of basic need satisfaction which 'provides the basis of the obligation to provide welfare' (Plant *et al.* 1980: 93). From this point of view, the entitlement to basic need satisfaction is a right. This position implies that rights can be expressed in substantive terms, and in our framework this means in terms of the desired outcomes which should be achieved for all individuals. This conception of substantive rights differs from that propounded by Coote (1993) which refers to rights to services and facilities, being consistent with our notion of needs as desired outcomes. However, the notion of substantive rights would be difficult to enforce because of problems defining the desired outcomes in precise, unambiguous terms and because of the inevitable need to establish priorities for scarce resources. As Coote (1993: 11–12) argues: 'It is hard to see how substantive rights which depend upon publicly-funded intervention (unless severely limited) can be enforced effectively while public resources are limited.'

A further potential problem with the substantive notion of rights is a tendency to neglect the issue of citizen participation in decisions on welfare; indeed, there is an implication of a 'centralist' approach to the determination of rights in terms of standards of basic need satisfaction. This criticism is levelled by Doyal and Gough (1992: 138–9) at Rawls's theory of justice which relates rights to the satisfaction of basic human needs; it is argued that social justice requires an additional 'participatory principle' involving the diffusion of political power and the provision of opportunities for maximum citizen participation in defining and implementing needs-based policies.

These problems with substantive rights have led to the advocacy of procedural rights – the rights 'to fair treatment of individuals as they come into contact (or try to come into contact) with service providers' (Coote 1992: 2). Such rights include the right to a fair hearing, to equal and consistent treatment, to unbiased decisions, to adherence to explicit guidelines in discretionary decisions, to information on the rationale for decisions, and to complaint, redress and appeal (Coote 1993: 12). Although such rights address the issue of participation in decision making, they do not relate directly to substantive needs and therefore embody a limited notion of social justice. Indeed, in themselves they can be regarded as providing only partial empowerment of citizens relative to a notion of citizenship that requires the equalization of life chances. Consequently, there is a danger of procedural rights playing a legitimatory role, giving the appearance of a basis for the achievement of social justice yet failing to address the key issue of the distribution of substantive welfare outcomes and the nature of the policies and political choices which determine such distribution. As indicated earlier, the *Citizen's Charter*'s (HMSO 1991) approach to consumer rights can be criticized on these grounds.

Notwithstanding this criticism, it is clear that procedural rights can play an important role in supplementing substantive rights relating to need satisfaction given the difficulties of operationalizing the latter. Of particular importance is the issue of participation in, and influence over, decision making and in this sense the notion of procedural rights is related to that of 'voice'; indeed, the right to effective voice can be seen as just such a procedural right.

Citizen empowerment through voice

In order to ensure that the definition of needs and the desired overall level of need satisfaction (and hence the degree of social justice achieved) are politically negotiated through the full involvement of all relevant stakeholders, strategies are required to empower citizens to participate in, and exercise appropriate influence over, decision making in public services. Empowerment in these terms is clearly important to the promotion of citizenship; it produces better outcomes in terms of need satisfaction through involving in decision making those directly affected by the decisions; it enables citizens to protect themselves and their group against tyranny by others; it encourages self-development and a capacity for political judgement; and it guarantees the equal dignity of all citizens (Doyal and Gough 1992: 138–9).

The traditional approach to considering public participation in decision making is through the 'normal' channels of representative democracy. However, this is subject to severe limitations as a means of providing citizens with effective voice. First, there are problems in the ability of citizens to influence decision making via elected representatives. Many people do not know who their local MP and councillors are; the characteristics of the latter rarely reflect the social composition of the population they serve; and they have limited time to take up the views of their constituents (Hambleton and Hoggett 1993: 109). Second, there are problems in the ability of elected representatives to monitor effectively and hold to account the behaviour of professionals; there is both asymmetry of information (professionals have better knowledge and experience) and asymmetry of motivation (professionals have greater incentive to limit their accountability) (Plant 1992: 27–8).

Consequently, effective voice strategies require more radical forms of participatory and direct democracy to shift power from producer interests to all citizens, whether as individuals or collectively in groups, who have an interest in the decisions in question. Various means have been proposed to achieve such a shift in power and an ascent of the 'ladder of participation': issue voting, referendums, citizens' juries, user panels, customer surveys, consultation documents, neighbourhood committees, cooption on to council committees, etc. However, the actual achievement of a shift in power is notoriously difficult to achieve, as Sinfield (1980: 177) argued:

> But any real shift of power to the service recipient is notoriously hard to obtain. Far from steadily ascending . . . the 'ladder of citizen participation', poor clients are likely to be submerged, taken over, or cooled out . . .
> In societies marked by differences of class, religion, or race that tend to separate planners and providers from the public service clients in greatest need, the sharing of power by the dominant groups is not likely to come about easily.

Decentralization, empowerment and effectiveness

Much has been written about the potential of decentralization, particularly in the local government context, to achieve the required shift in power (Hoggett and Hambleton 1987; Hambleton and Hoggett 1993; Burns *et al.* 1994). Thus Burns *et al.* (1994: xiv) argue that decentralization 'has the potential not only to provide responsive, high-quality services, but also a range of possibilities for strengthening citizen involvement in the governing process'. Hambleton and Hoggett (1993: 110–11) argue, in the local government context, that decentralization is the basis for citizen empowerment through voice:

> A fully democratic local government necessitates a radically devolved administrative structure in which service managers and local user and community groups have real power over resources and the freedom to bend central policies to local circumstances and even create local strategies . . . it requires the ability to tolerate a much greater degree of political and organisational pluralism than has existed in the past.

Thus decentralization is seen as the key to promoting effective participation by communities in decision making and enhancing accountability of public institutions and organizations to those communities. However, it also has two other advantages in relation to our model of needs-based public services. First, the localization of service provision provides the potential to adapt policies and services more closely to the needs of communities provided that powers of decision making and control over resources are devolved so that local discretion can be exercised in identifying needs and priorities and adapting policies and services to local circumstances. Second, decentralization can enhance the prospect for coordination between services, both within multipurpose organizations such as local authorities and between local agencies. As argued above, this provides a better basis for identifying and addressing needs which require complex and integrated policy and service responses (Burns *et al.* 1994: 85–104).

Therefore, through devolution of power, localization and integration the potential for the development of needs-based public services is seen as maximized in a decentralized context. However, the realization of this potential is dependent upon a number of significant barriers being overcome, for example professional and political reluctance to devolve power from the centre and 'departmentalism' and barriers to interagency collaboration. In particular, the devolution of control over resources is crucial to allow localities to develop strategies, adapt policies and reallocate resources in accordance with locally negotiated needs and priorities. It is essential to develop effective means whereby the participation of individuals, groups and communities in decision making can be secured which confer meaningful power upon them and promote a pluralistic approach within which particular special interests are unable to dominate. Clearly, the achievement of these requirements implies a radical change in current forms of social and political organization.

Within such a decentralized framework of public service provision, there will inevitably be significant local variation in the application of policies, the way in which services are delivered and in the standards of service provided. This will be necessary to increase the overall effectiveness of public services since the focus is on achieving locally variable desired outcomes rather than on providing uniform service outputs. Therefore it will be necessary to manage a tension between local discretion and variability on the one hand and a central concern with broader consistency and fairness on the other. Clearly, dangers of abuses of power and 'capture' by sectional interests arise due to decentralization and some central control is needed to prevent these abuses. Moreover, the centre would retain responsibility for developing a corporate strategic policy framework and, in this context, setting minimum standards in relation to certain outcomes which are regarded as the right of all citizens.

Conclusion

The concept of need is inherently contestable, embodying a commitment to some form of collective welfare provision which will be rejected by proponents of market liberalism. This dispute is more about values than empirical evidence revolving around different perspectives on the role of individuals relative to social structures and institutions as agents of social change. After over 15 years of government policies which have sought to 'roll back the state' and enhance the scope of the market in determining economic and social outcomes, fundamental questions are being asked about the role of the state and the extent to which individuals should be responsible for the welfare of themselves and their families.

We have presented a critique of the economic liberalism of the New Right position arguing that market failures undermine the technical and social efficiency of market outcomes, and that inequalities generated by markets, far from being natural and inevitable, are products of a political, social and institutional context which is morally contestable. We have emphasized the ideological nature of New Right thinking. The acknowledgement of a limited role for the state to address 'externalities', 'special needs', and 'limited inequalities' serves to reinforce the notion that there are no fundamental flaws in the normal operation of the market which require radical change in economic and social relations. State action to address social needs is marginalized as 'external' to and separate from the operation of the market; such needs are presented as capable of treatment without addressing market forces.

Moreover, where state action is required, the emphasis on choice (or exit) as the means to promoting efficiency provides merely an appearance of consumer empowerment and depoliticizes the relationship between the state and citizens by reducing it to the individualistic notion of economic exchange. Political approaches to empowerment involving collective action are invalidated. Action by citizens is a matter of consultation or complaint in relation to specific services; the underlying policies and political choices are protected from challenge.

This critique is premised upon an alternative conception of the desirable form of economic and social organization. This alternative position advocates collective action to achieve social outcomes radically different from those achieved through the market system. This is seen as justified on the grounds of both allocative efficiency (to 'correct' market failures) and distributive justice, rejecting the notion of Paretian social efficiency and asserting the need to address explicitly the extent to which the distribution of income and wealth conforms to notions of social justice.

In developing a model for effective public service provision, we focus on the relationship of the concept of need to social problems and outcomes. We argue that needs-based public policy must be focused on outcomes, the basic purpose of collective action being to achieve effectively (and efficiently) those outcomes which are socially perceived as most valued in relation to the diagnosis of social problems and the valuation of social ends. Within this perspective, it is argued that the achievement of outcomes consistent with notions of social justice may require radical policies which seek to change the basic economic and social relations of market society. We also argue that the effectiveness of such collective action is contingent upon democratization to provide citizens with 'voice'. Thus it is necessary to ensure that the definition of needs (as desired outcomes), priorities between them and the required overall level of need satisfaction (and hence the degree of social justice achieved) are politically negotiated through full participation of all stakeholders. This will require radical strategies based upon collective notions of citizenship which decentralize power to communities and promote forms of direct democracy.

Therefore, in advocating a society in which democratically based collective action is justified in terms of the promotion of social justice through public policies and services which achieve desired social outcomes effectively, we are arguing for radical change in forms of economic, social and political organization. In this sense, discussion of the concept of need and its role in the public policy process cannot be confined to a narrow 'technical' basis. We are necessarily dealing with fundamental political, even philosophical issues which are the subject of perennial controversy: the kind of society we wish to achieve; the nature of desirable social outcomes and priorities; the relative status and potentials of individual and collective action; the form of economic and social processes and organization which will best secure desired outcomes; the nature of government action required to promote effective achievement of such outcomes; the characteristics of democratic processes of political negotiation which will maximize accountability of the state to 'empowered citizens'.

Note

1 Social efficiency requires that the social benefits of a policy exceed its social costs and the assumption is made that the distribution of costs and benefits is irrelevant. The concept of Pareto efficiency is employed in welfare economics to deal with the problem of differential valuation by individuals of costs and benefits. Thus, a Pareto-optimal resource allocation is deemed to exist when it is not possible to make further changes to benefit one person without reducing the welfare of someone else. The concept can be extended by applying the so-called Kaldor-Hicks Compensation Principle which states that if the beneficiaries from a policy can compensate the losers and retain a net benefit then that policy will result in a Pareto improvement in welfare (Pearce and Nash 1981; Levacic 1987).

References

Barry, N. (1987) Understanding the market. In M. Loney, R. Bocock, J. Clarke, A. Cochrane, P. Graham and M. Wilson (eds) *The State or the Market? Politics and Welfare in Contemporary Britain*. London: Sage.

Bradshaw, J. (1972) The concept of social need, *New Society*, 30 March: 640–3.

Burns, D., Hambleton, R. and Hoggett, P. (1994) *The Politics of Decentralisation: Revitalising Local Democracy*. Basingstoke: Macmillan.

Charles, S.T. and Webb, A.L. (1986) *The Economic Approach to Social Policy*. Brighton: Wheatsheaf Books.

Clapham, D. and Smith, S.J. (1990) Housing policy and 'special needs', *Policy and Politics*, 18 (3): 193–205.

Coote, A. (ed.) (1992) *The Welfare of Citizens: Developing New Social Rights*. London: IPPR/Rivers Oram Press.

Coote, A. (1993) *Bridging the Gap Between 'Them' and 'Us': Notes on Power and Participation in a Modern Welfare Democracy*. London: IPPR.

Culyer, A.J. (1980) *The Political Economy of Social Policy*. Oxford: Martin Robertson.

Donnison, D. (1994) *Act Local: Social Justice from the Bottom Up*. London: IPPR.

Doyal, L. and Gough, I. (1991) *A Theory of Human Need*. London: Macmillan.

Glennerster, H. (1983) *Planning for Priority Groups*. Oxford: Martin Robertson.

Hambleton, R. and Hoggett, P. (1993) Rethinking consumerism in public services, *Consumer Policy Review*, 3 (2): 103–11.

Hill, M. and Bramley, G. (1986) *Analysing Social Policy*. Oxford: Basil Blackwell.

Hills, J. (1995) *Inquiry into Income and Wealth, Volume II: A Summary of the Evidence*. York: Joseph Rowntree Foundation.

HMSO (1991) *The Citizen's Charter: Raising the Standard*, Cm 1599. London: HMSO.

Hoggett, P. and Hambleton, R. (eds) (1987) *Decentralisation and Democracy: Localising Public Services*, Occasional Paper No. 28, School for Advanced Urban Studies, University of Bristol.

Johnson, N. (1990) *Reconstructing the Welfare State: A Decade of Change 1980–1990*. London: Harvester Wheatsheaf.

King, D.S. (1987) *The New Right: Politics, Markets and Citizenship*. Basingstoke: Macmillan.

Knapp, M. (1984) *The Economics of Social Care*. London: Macmillan.

LeGrand, J. (1982) *The Strategy of Equality*. London: George Allen and Unwin.

LeGrand, J. and Robinson, R. (1984) *The Economics of Social Problems: The Market versus the State*. Basingstoke: Macmillan.

Levacic, R. (1987) *Economic Policy-Making: Its Theory and Practice*. Brighton: Wheatsheaf.

Marks, D. (1995) Evaluating the reforms: Balancing act, *Health Service Journal*, 105 (5448): 26–7.

Minford, P. (1987) The role of the social services: A view from the New Right. In M. Loney, R. Bocock, J. Clarke, A. Cochrane, P. Graham and M. Wilson (eds) *The State or the Market? Politics and Welfare in Contemporary Britain*. London: Sage.

Mishra, R. (1984) *The Welfare State in Crisis*. Brighton: Wheatsheaf.

Pearce, D.W. and Nash, C.A. (1981) *The Social Appraisal of Projects: A Text in Cost–Benefit Analysis*. London: Macmillan.

Phillips, M. (1995) Time's up for the welfare state, *Observer*, 14 May.

Plant, R. (1992) Citizenship, rights and welfare. In A. Coote (ed.) *The Welfare of Citizens: Developing New Social Rights*. London: IPPR/Rivers Oram Press.

Plant, R., Lesser, H. and Taylor-Gooby, P. (1980) *Political Philosophy and Social Welfare: Essays on the Normative Basis of Welfare Provision*. London: Routledge and Kegan Paul.

Pollitt, C. (1988) Bringing consumers into performance measurement: Concepts, consequences and constraints, *Policy and Politics*, 16 (2): 77–87.

Pollitt, C. and Harrison, S. (1992) *Handbook of Public Service Management*. Oxford: Blackwell.

Ranade, W. and Haywood, S. (1989) Privatizing from within: The National Health Service under Thatcher, *Local Government Studies*, July/August: 19–34.

Self, P. (1993) *Government by the Market? The Politics of Public Choice*. Basingstoke: Macmillan.

Sinfield, A. (1980) Meeting client need: An ambiguous and precarious value. In D. Grunow and F. Hegner (eds) *Welfare or Bureaucracy? Problems of Matching Social Services to Client Needs* Volume II. Cambridge, MA: Oelgescheager, Gunn and Hain.

Taylor-Gooby, P. and Dale, J. (1981) *Social Theory and Social Welfare*. London: Edward Arnold.

Walker, A. (1984) *Social Planning: A Strategy for Socialist Welfare*. Oxford: Basil Blackwell.

Weir, S. and Hall, W. (1994) *Ego Trip: Extra-Governmental Organisations in the UK and their Accountability*. London: Democratic Audit, University of Essex and Charter 88 Trust.

Williams, F. (1989) *Social Policy: A Critical Introduction*. Cambridge: Polity Press.

Wistow, G., Knapp, M., Hardy, B. and Allen, C. (1994) *Social Care in a Mixed Economy*. Buckingham: Open University Press.

METHODOLOGIES FOR NEEDS ASSESSMENT

Introduction

As the case studies in the second part of this volume illustrate, needs assessments in Great Britain are nowadays undertaken in a variety of contexts by different agencies and for many reasons. Not surprisingly the ways in which needs are assessed also vary a great deal. As we shall see, an assessment of need can be carried out by a civil servant working alone, with access to government statistics and perhaps the help of a microcomputer. Alternatively, a needs assessment might be based on group discussions by users of a service to define and highlight their own needs. Such diverse methods need not be mutually exclusive. Increasingly, a range of techniques are adopted to provide more than one form of measurement and to obtain different perspectives on an issue.

This chapter provides an overview of methods currently used in needs assessments, drawing on examples from across the public sector. The emphasis is less on the technical details of different approaches than the methodological principles (stated or otherwise) which guide them. The actual mechanics of undertaking a survey of housing needs, for example, are not addressed here. Rather, we are concerned with the rationale for and implications of doing such a survey as compared say, with an assessment of housing need based on local authority housing waiting lists.

The discussion is organized as follows. In the first section we review a range of methods for assessing need from the interpretation of existing information to more direct approaches involving the collection of new information through, for example, surveys and focus group discussions. The advantages and disadvantages associated with these different methods are considered next with reference to the contextual, practical and philosophical issues which impinge upon the needs assessment process. Finally we look at methodologies which incorporate a variety of methods and therefore offer, it is argued, the most appropriate means of understanding the multidimensional character of need.

Methods for needs assessment

The assessment of needs requires the collation, collection and analysis of information. This information may be derived from a range of different sources and take a number of different forms. For the purpose of this discussion we look at two different types of information that are commonly used in needs assessment: existing (or secondary) information and new (or primary) information.

Analyses of existing information

Routinely collected statistical information represents a vast body of facts and figures which can be analysed and interpreted so as to provide an indication of aggregate levels of need. The importance of such information in terms of its impact on public life can be seen when we consider that such indicators and indices are used by central government to determine the amount of block grant to be allocated to local authorities, or within the health service, to allocate resources to district health authorities each year. Sophisticated technology means that data can be collected from diverse sources to provide pictures of need at local and national levels, which reflect geographic variations and differences between social groups.

An important example is the *Index of Local Conditions* developed by the Department of the Environment. Introduced as a measure of 'relative levels of deprivation across all areas of England' (DoE 1994: 3), the index combines a number of indicators from the 1991 census of population and other sources (including, for example, the Benefits Agency and the Department for Education) to produce deprivation scores for areas at local authority district, ward and census enumeration district (ED) levels. At the local authority district level, three measures are produced to show: the degree of deprivation for the whole area relative to other areas, the extent of deprivation across the area (i.e. the proportion of EDs within the area which are deprived) and the intensity or severity of deprivation within the area. The 366 local authority districts are ranked according to their scores for each of these measures. Thus, for example, Solihull is ranked at 223 (of 366) in terms of the overall degree of deprivation, at 60 in terms of the extent of deprivation, and at 50 in terms of the intensity of deprivation. The *Index of Local Conditions* is composed of 13 indicators 'chosen to cover a range of economic, social, housing and environmental issues' (DoE 1994: 3). These indicators include unemployment, overcrowding, non-car ownership, educational participation, standardized mortality rates, house contents insurance premiums and derelict land. The selection of alternative variables represents the principal difference between indices of these types and reflects the purpose for which they are intended. This point can be seen by comparing the DoE's *Index* with that compiled by Jarman to identify likely levels of general practitioner (GP) workload in particular areas (Jarman 1983). Amongst Jarman's indicators are the proportion of children aged under five, lone pensioners, recently arrived immigrants and ethnic minorities. Whilst it makes sense for Jarman to include these population groups because they tend to make higher than average demands on GP services, it would be inappropriate to include them in the deprivation index, since only some members of these groups will actually be deprived.

The basic approach deployed by Jarman and the DoE has been deployed in numerous studies of deprivation at local levels in an attempt to obtain a more comprehensive picture of social need and disadvantage. The *Southwark Poverty Profile*, for example, utilized five groups of indicators under the headings of financial, personal, household, housing condition and educational priority to identify specific areas of the borough affected by a particular problem and 'in conjunction to form an aggregated picture of multiple deprivation across the borough' (London Borough of Southwark 1987: 7). This picture was complemented in the study in two ways. First, by mapping secondary indicators relating to the provision of services and facilities, the authors were able to assess to what extent resources were currently being directed towards areas of greatest need. Second, by reviewing other reports on poverty in the borough, 'perceptions' of what it means to be poor were included thus adding a qualitative dimension to what is essentially a quantitative analysis.

Whereas a wide range of indicators was used in Southwark, *The Kirklees Social Needs Map* used a single indicator, community charge benefits data (Reeve 1991). Essentially, the author calculated the percentage of residents in the area who were in receipt of either maximum or some benefit and disaggregated these figures to show concentrations of highest poverty down to postcode level and the extent of poverty across the area. The important point to note here is that a single indicator is being used as a proxy for poverty.

Both the Southwark and Kirklees profiles focus on urban deprivation. In a study of rural deprivation prepared for the Convention of Scottish Local Authorities, Midwinter and Monaghan (1990) argue that deprivation is unlikely to be as geographically concentrated in rural areas as it is in towns and cities but will tend to be experienced by particular groups in the population. The authors' selection and analysis of existing information is designed to pick up aspects of rural deprivation such as poor access to services, the importance of which, they believe, other studies have underestimated. Interregional comparisons made on the basis of commonly used social indicators are supplemented with five community case studies. The case studies, the authors claim, 'permit a more dynamic interpretation of the manifestations of deprivation by allowing a consideration of the interaction between need and service provision' (Midwinter and Monaghan 1990: 69).

Returning to an urban context, a more recent study in Newham shows how statistical data can be manipulated so as to highlight the needs of specific population groups or certain geographical areas. In a study of young people in Newham (Newham Youth Services 1994), existing data were used to highlight the problems facing young people in the borough. The profile was then used to project future levels of need and, consequently, to argue the case for increased resources:

> The population pyramids show that Newham has a substantially different pattern to England and Wales as a whole; whereas they have an 'ageing'

population, Newham has a young population. Distribution and provision of facilities need to reflect this.

(Newham Youth Services 1994: 32)

The traditional epidemiological approach to needs assessment used within the National Health Service also relies on existing information relating to the 'incidence and prevalence' of disease and availability and effectiveness of services. The sources of information for this type of assessment include census data and other sources already referred to but also health service utilization rates and selected morbidity statistics such as the cancer registry and infectious disease notifications. The logic for this kind of assessment differs from those previously discussed which identify needs with either people or places. Here, as the discussion paper points out, the methodology outlined rests on the assumption that 'needs are best described in terms of *disease boundaries* (e.g. the needs for services for diabetes)' (NHS Management Executive 1991b: 6).

Existing information, as this brief summary has shown, can be used to indicate comparative levels of need experienced by different groups or in different geographic areas, or to project needs for a service or facility. What each of these examples share is a reliance on information originally collected for purposes other than the direct assessment of need. Where they differ is in the selection and interpretation of that information, as this varies according to how need is conceptualized and defined. This choice, or dilemma, also informs the more direct forms of needs assessment to which we now turn.

The collection of new information on needs

The limitations of using existing data as a means of assessing needs at a local level are being increasingly recognized. As a result those responsible for carrying out needs assessments in a number of policy areas are using quantitative and qualitative research techniques to collect new (or primary) data about local populations.

Perhaps the most common technique in this regard is the social survey. Surveys are used to collect information in a standard format from a sample of individuals who are representative of a wider population. Surveys most obviously reveal numbers – the number of people who have used health or legal services, the number of people with a certain type of qualification, the number of people who have been victims of crime. These numbers can be analysed to show differences between people and places or to show the relative strength of feeling about different issues – forty per cent of women but only 20 per cent of men said that facilities for children are inadequate, or 61 per cent of respondents said that burglary was the most serious problem, 29 per cent that litter was the most serious and so on. Depending on the sorts of questions asked in a survey, qualitative information can also be collected – how could bus services be improved or why is the bus service so good. To demonstrate how surveys can be used in needs assessments, here are three examples, relating to housing, training, and health needs respectively.

Ryedale District Council undertook a major household survey in 1992 to identify areas of greatest housing need in the district and to enable it to direct its capital investment programme accordingly. In order to maximize the amount of information collected at subdistrict level in a largely rural area, the council opted for a postal survey of housing need rather than relying on a smaller sample and conducting face to face interviews. This method allowed 10 per cent of households in larger areas and 40 per cent of households in smaller areas to be surveyed, producing a sample of over 8000 households, approximately 20 per cent of the total number in the area. As is common for self-completion questionnaires, almost all questions were closed, allowing only quantitative analysis to be conducted. The *depth* of information about the nature of housing need was, in this case, limited in order to ensure *breadth* of information about different geographic areas (Van Zijl 1993).

The Skill Needs In Britain – 1993 survey (IFF Research Ltd 1993) was the fourth in a series of telephone surveys of employers conducted for the Department of Employment which were designed to identify training needs and related concerns at a national level. Interviews were conducted with representatives from over 4000 establishments employing 25 or more employees across the public and private sector and in different regions. The survey addressed difficulties employers have or expect to have filling vacancies, the amount of training being undertaken and the quality of that training, and existing skill levels in relation to the skill needs of the organization. All of the information collected in the study either came as or was transformed into, hard, quantified data, enabling statistical comparisons to be made of the training needs of organizations in different sectors of the economy, in different regions and of different sizes. The survey followed the same format as in previous years' studies allowing for changes over time to be documented as well.

The third example is a survey undertaken by the West Lambeth Health Authority Community Unit in the late 1980s. The household survey formed part of a wider project, the aims of which were to explore perceptions of health and health needs – comparing those of lay people and professionals – and to examine the implications for health related planning. The survey comprised a representative sample of 227 interviews conducted face to face with individuals in their own homes. Unlike the surveys of housing and training needs, many of the questions in this survey were open ended, enabling people, the author says, 'to redefine health and their own health needs' (Dun 1989: 5). The responses were subsequently coded, allowing for some quantitative analysis including comparisons along the lines of class, tenure, age, etc.

The key difference between the three surveys is that in the first two examples, the research was conducted with a fixed view of housing and skill needs respectively and aimed to establish where and in what numbers such needs existed, whereas the third survey was in part about discovering people's health needs as they themselves perceived them. The rationale behind the West Lambeth survey underpins more qualitative research techniques such as unstructured interviews and focus groups, some examples of which are now considered.

Whereas surveys of the kind described above are used to collect relatively small amounts of information from relatively large groups of individuals, the principle behind unstructured or qualitative interviewing is the reverse. How many individuals say this or that is relatively unimportant; the point of the interview is rather to find out why someone adopts a particular perspective or feels the way they do. In practice unstructured interviews are frequently used to complement the findings of a survey and to add depth to the information revealed, often with regard to particular groups. In a study of the skills and training needs of residents in a relatively deprived district of Merseyside, qualitative interviews were undertaken in just such a way. An interview survey of 2000 individuals was followed up by in-depth interviews with a small number from the original sample selected because they seemed to face particular barriers to finding work or training. The survey revealed, for example, that a lack of childcare facilities was a significant problem for lone parents. The in-depth interviews were designed to discover what such problems actually meant for lone parents and to begin to identify potential solutions to them (Policy Research Unit 1993).

Like qualitative interviews, focus groups are often used as a means of exploring in further depth issues arising from a survey. Groups usually involve individuals with shared experiences such as young or old people, the long term unemployed or people with disabilities. Or, alternatively, they may be carefully constructed to be representative of a given population. In a study of community involvement in a community health needs assessment project, groups convened 'included school students and teachers, parents, males and females, employed and unemployed, disabled people, tertiary students and staff, health providers and service groups' (Knox and Chapman 1995: 113). Describing their role in the study, the authors say that focus groups 'were considered to be an appropriate way of encouraging open discussion about health issues, experiences with health services and aspects of life in the community' (Knox and Chapman 1995: 113). Focus groups differ from qualitative interviews with individuals because they bring together different perspectives on issues and can generate new ideas and insights through the process of discussion and debate.

Generating new ideas might also be the objective of public meetings used in the needs assessment process. Unlike focus groups which are controlled in the sense that specific individuals are invited to participate in a discussion, public meetings are open and anyone can attend. A study of community health and welfare needs in Leeds followed a postal survey of local residents, in-depth follow-up interviews and qualitative interviews with local representatives and service providers, with a series of open public meetings 'at which these two perspectives . . . could be summarised, conflicts of opinion identified and a start made in agreeing on the needs which should be given a priority' (Percy-Smith and Sanderson 1992: 13).

Whilst it is common for focus groups to follow on from a survey, there is of course no rule about this. Group discussions were used, for example, to inform the design of questionnaires in a needs assessment relating to recreational facilities conducted by the University of Illinois. The group's aim was to ensure that the questionnaires were phrased in everyday language and that the subsequent survey findings would reflect users' perceptions of leisure services and not be distorted by academic preconceptions of the issues. Three sets of groups were organized: stakeholders such as staff and board members, groups with special recreational interests and randomly selected members of the community.

> Each group served different purposes. The groups made up of staff and board members provided useful information about the activities offered by the programs being evaluated ... The groups made up of the special interest people could provide in depth discussions about specific needs of the community in terms of specialised recreation and leisure opportunities. Finally, the general public groups could provide information that was relatively unclouded by institutional or special interest concerns.
>
> (Mitra 1994: 135)

The author also notes that an indirect benefit of focus groups is that they can raise awareness about the service being provided and in this case generate publicity about the survey, thus maximizing the response rate.

Just as focus groups can be conducted before surveys to inform the process of questionnaire design, unstructured interviews can similarly help to develop a feel for key issues and/or to identify terms and phrases which are commonly used by service users, as opposed to the technical jargon of service providers. A community needs audit conducted in Leeds began with informal interviews with key local players, including community representatives and service providers, in order to identify, in broad terms, issues of relevance to the area and highlight any specific problems which could then be addressed in the household survey (Policy Research Unit 1994). A slightly different purpose underpinned the outreach work of a community development worker in a health needs assessment undertaken in southeast London. Here the objective was to 'find out the subjective health concerns of local people' with the result that in the subsequent survey, 'bio-medical classification had to be rejected in favour of a system that was more meaningful to lay people' (Wainwright 1994: 29).

Thus far we have seen how focus groups and unstructured interviews have been used in conjunction with surveys in needs assessments. In a study of the links between unemployment and health needs in a community in north Derbyshire, unstructured interviews were used exclusively. The project was based on a methodology first developed by anthropologists in an international development context known as 'participatory rapid appraisal'. Underlying this approach is a concern that traditional research has a tendency to work *on* people when what is required to gain a full understanding from research is to work *with* people. Participation in the research process is of paramount concern and a range of techniques are utilized and modified with this in mind. In the north Derbyshire project, interviews were held both with key people (service professionals, elected councillors, shopkeepers, community leaders) and members of the community who represented different interests and concerns (different age groups, men and women, etc.). The interviews were focused around 'questions based on the differences between perceptions of the community and those of health professionals about the health problems of the area' (Cresswell 1992: 28) and used props such as maps to help people point out problem areas on the estate in question. A distinctive feature of this approach was that interviewees had their responses to questions repeated back to them and were asked to check and change (if necessary) the information they provided. In this way, Cresswell (1992: 29) argues, she worked 'as a catalyst for their ideas, they have done the thinking'.

There is a wide range of methods available for collecting new information on needs and the choice of methods has several implications. The methods chosen dictate, for example, whether the information is mostly quantitative or qualitative and whether it relates to individuals or groups. Who participates in the assessment and in what way is also determined, as is the extent to which it forms part of a process of actually meeting need. Many of these issues have been implicit in this review of methods currently employed in needs assessments, but the discussion now moves on to a more explicit discussion of their relative advantages and disadvantages, and of their appropriateness in different contexts.

Methodological issues

In order to illustrate the distinctive aspects of various methods used in needs assessments, and the range of contexts in which they apply, the previous discussion tended to treat them in isolation, as if the methods could be and are used exclusively. Whilst this can be the case and indeed was so with the examples of studies relying on existing information, in practice many needs assessments involve a combination of techniques. Before looking at some examples of more rounded assessments, however, it is useful to consider the relative advantages and disadvantages of these methods. In so doing, we address contextual issues – those relating to the purpose of the assessment; practical issues, such as the availability of time and money; and, most importantly, philosophical issues around how need is conceptualized.

Using existing information provides a cost-effective and relatively quick means of drawing attention to the comparative needs of different population groups whether they be defined spatially or along such lines as gender, age or ethnicity. Simply because of the amount of information available, such analyses are likely to offer more wide-ranging indicators of need than assessments involving the collection of new data. The development of geographic information systems means that maps can be drawn showing areas with high numbers of people on benefits, or with different levels of overcrowding or of car ownership and so on, providing a graphic illustration of relative deprivation at national, regional or local levels. Existing information can be used to provide temporal comparisons as well, showing trends over time and projecting future levels of need. Information collected regularly can be relatively reliable; census data and data from surveys undertaken regularly at a national level, for example, is collected systematically with great care to ensure that they elicit responses that are consistent year on year and between individuals.

On the whole, however, there are more problems and limitations with analyses of existing information than there are benefits and possibilities. First, because it is usually collected for purposes other than needs assessment, there is no guarantee that existing information will reflect actual need, a point made here in relation to social indices such as the *Index of Local Conditions* (DoE 1994) and Jarman's index:

> Indicators are only surrogates, proxies, of possibly unmeasurable phenomena. For example, the census of population results for households lacking two basic amenities, such as exclusive use of a bath or WC, are supposed to 'represent' poor housing. But can these data be used to indicate areas of poor quality housing? A condemned tower block with damp, asbestos ridden flats will not show up as poor housing using this indicator if all flats have exclusive facilities.
>
> (Hawtin *et al.* 1994: 66)

A related and perhaps more serious problem is that existing information tells us little about need beyond the fact that it appears to exist. This problem was tackled to some extent in *The Southwark Poverty Profile* (London Borough of Southwark 1987) and the study of rural deprivation in Scotland (Midwinter and Monaghan 1990) discussed earlier which referred to secondary sources that could provide a qualitative dimension in the form, for example, of quotations from people experiencing poverty. However, this remains generalized information and cannot be more than a basis for more in-depth assessments targeted at specific issues as the authors of these studies readily admit. Statistical generalizations, we might note here, can result in what is known in social research as the 'ecological fallacy', whereby the characteristics of an area or group are assumed to be equally shared by individuals in it, rather than distributed differentially as is usually the case.

Practical difficulties with analyses of existing information include the fact that it can be very dated. Consider for instance that census data is only collected every 10 years. Also problematic is the fact that different kinds of information will relate to different geographical boundaries – postcode areas, electoral wards, school or GP catchment areas, etc. – and may therefore be incompatible.

Finally, there is the fact that analyses of this kind usually require some sort of statistical expertise and even technical knowledge specific to the data source. As an illustration, much of the information used in epidemiological assessments is 'codified', its meaning and meaningfulness the domain of health professionals. Not only does this result in the information representing a 'black box', supposedly explaining everything but obscure to the public, but it also reflects the professionals' perspective or 'world view'. With epidemiological assessments, known 'incidence and prevalence rates' and existing services are the benchmark for measuring needs. In a different context, using waiting lists as a sole indicator of housing need would reflect a similar institutional bias.

This last problem is also evident in needs assessments for social care undertaken through structured interviews by welfare professionals. Although the move towards care in the community is predicated in part on the view that care services should be needs rather than service-led, the *Care Management and*

Assessment: Practitioner's Guide is clear that ultimately 'the assessing practitioner is responsible for defining the user's needs' and for deciding 'the eligibility of users for assistance from their own agency' (Department of Health 1991: 53). These are theoretically distinct judgements; it is incumbent on the assessor to identify needs which cannot be met as well as those that can. Nonetheless, the potential for practitioners to steer the assessment in a direction in which they know a service response can be made is clear. This partly depends on how need is defined by the practitioner, as Richards has pointed out:

> Separating the assessment of needs from a subsequent decision about eligibility depends in fact on the concept of need being operationalised independently of the agency policies and guidelines that are to determine what is to count as need, and this is where the difficulty lies. For unless such a separation can be maintained, the distinction between service-led and needs-based assessment becomes much less meaningful.
>
> (Richards 1994: 6)

If the practitioner's perception of need merely corresponds with his or her agency's existing eligibility criteria, then the problem of the 'expert' defining the user's needs is unlikely to be challenged and so new, more responsive services are, correspondingly, unlikely to emerge. In practice, the problem may be less one of contested conceptions of need and more a question of financial or administrative constraints. Reporting on her observations of needs assessments, Richards notes that: 'The needs of an elderly person wishing to remain in the community, for example, are only met if the cost of the care package does not exceed the cost to the local authority of residential care' (1994: 8).

A more detailed examination of these issues is made in Chapter 4, on needs assessments for community care. For our purposes here, the main point is that where professionals have joint responsibility for assessing need for a service and delivering that service, this can distort the former in favour of the latter both because of difficulties in the definition of need and because of the strong organizational and financial constraints on actual service delivery. These considerations need to be set against the apparent advantage of needs assessments conducted in this way which, somewhat ironically, is that professionals, precisely because they understand how services operate, are best placed to know whether and in what way an individual's needs can be met.

Turning to the use of surveys in needs assessments, the first point to be made is that different types of survey have advantages and disadvantages in relation to each other. This was implicit in the above discussion. The postal survey of housing needs in a rural context was appropriate because a large sample was required to make meaningful comparisons at a small area level and postal surveys are relatively inexpensive to administer. The telephone survey of the training needs of organizations, being a national study, also involved a large sample but here a postal survey would have been problematic. Responses needed to be secured from the 'right' person (someone with responsibility for training) and whereas there is very little guarantee that this will happen with mailed out questionnaires, a telephone interviewer can track them down. The two surveys differed from the third example in that they collected predominantly quantitative information. To collect qualitative information, it is in general best to conduct interviews face to face so that questions can be clarified and followed up with probes. This was, as we saw, a crucial element of the health needs survey which was designed to investigate different perceptions of need.

Notwithstanding the fact that surveys can be used to obtain different kinds of information, their principal merit lies with their generalizability and this does apply more to quantitative than qualitative data. Provided that certain conventions are followed with regard to sampling technique, questionnaire design and so on, the results of surveys can usually be taken to be representative of the population as a whole. However, this is both easier and more likely to be accurate if what is being reported are the responses to a closed question where the only responses available are those listed, than those to an open ended question where the range of possible answers is infinite and their meaning more subjective. So surveys are most appropriate where response categories can be pre-set, effectively limiting their range and depth but maximizing their statistical significance.

Where the participation of individuals is seen as an important part of the process of needs assessment, surveys are valuable because they will involve relatively large numbers of people. The size of a sample might reflect this concern. For example the needs audit in Leeds already referred to (Policy Research Unit 1994) was designed as an exercise in community development, as well as a means of identifying needs, and the size of the sample was consequently larger than was strictly necessary in statistical terms to make generalizations about the population as a whole or groups and areas within it. This aspect of surveys might also be seen as a disadvantage. Surveys for needs assessments involve asking people questions about what their needs are and how far they are being met. This can have the result of raising expectations in a situation where the aim and possibility is one of improved service provision but where the outcome is by no means certain.

Practical disadvantages with surveys are that even where the cheaper option is chosen (a small postal survey perhaps), they are not inexpensive, and they also take time to organize and undertake. At least some knowledge of the techniques involved (sampling, questionnaire design, interviewing, statistical analysis) is also necessary to ensure that the results do actually show what they claim to and that they are effectively used.

The main advantages of qualitative techniques were noted in the review of methods above. Unstructured interviews and focus group discussions can be used to explain the underlying reasons behind responses obtained in a survey or to inform survey design by establishing key issues or by finding out terms and phrases which are used in everyday life in reference to the subject at hand. In general these types of methods allow participants to express their ideas and feelings in their own way and there is less likelihood of their responses being framed to fit neat boxes designed by the assessor, a potential problem with surveys. This freedom of expression is particularly relevant with regard to needs assessment because of the contested nature of need.

Focus groups and public meetings have the additional advantage of being forums for debate where new ideas can be generated or where a consensus of opinion can be sought over issues which a survey may have revealed to be contentious. People in groups often react differently to issues from the way they would have reacted as inidividuals precisely because perspectives which they had not previously considered may be presented by other members.

Participatory rapid appraisal (PRA) is a research methodology which incorporates methods such as focus groups and unstructured interviews but which is especially applicable for community development, as this comment outlines:

> The main advantages of PRA over conventional survey research are its level of community participation, short duration and low costs ... It involves the field team and community members in all aspects of the study, the design of the research tools, the collection of information, and the analysis of the findings. Only data which will actually be used by development workers and community members in their work is collected, and a high degree of participation in the study guarantees that the information collected is relevant.
>
> (Theis and Grady 1991: 32)

The degree of community involvement appropriate in a needs assessment will of course depend upon its wider purpose. It makes no sense in some instances, such as a skill needs survey of employers, but is actually a specified aim in others, such as the previously mentioned needs audits in Leeds.

In practical terms, unstructured interviews and focus groups require different skills and resources to those needed to conduct a survey. They can be less expensive as fewer people are usually needed to administer them and the number of participants involved is generally less than for surveys. However, conducting an unstructured interview demands more skill than asking tickbox questions. Similarly, facilitating a focus group or public meeting requires knowledge of the subject matter, an ability to steer participants without stifling them and to manage the group in such a way that individuals have an equal opportunity to express their views. Getting people to attend focus groups and public meetings can be difficult because most are unused to such formal gatherings and are reluctant to put themselves in a situation requiring that they speak openly with strangers. This problem can be overcome with focus groups if they are organized around existing groups, but public meetings like the ones discussed earlier are notorious for being poorly attended.

Analysis of qualitative data is complicated and time consuming and whereas computers will perform most of the difficult tasks involved in statistical analysis, they are less adept at analysing words. Related to this problem, it is difficult to make generalizations on the basis of qualitative information either about issues or how different population groups feel about these issues. So although qualitative research methods do facilitate a broader understanding of need and especially its subjective dimension, they are less useful for measuring different levels of need and this might be the central aim of an assessment, for example to inform resource allocation.

None of the methods reviewed in this chapter, then, is without their problems and equally, all have something to offer the needs assessment process. Their suitability will vary according to the specific requirements of an assessment, the resources available and the way in which need is understood. Whilst these issues are not fixed, the arguments put forward in the opening chapters of this book suggest that need is a measurable, if complex and multidimensional, phenomenon. This discussion concludes with a brief examination of approaches which draw on diverse methods and thereby aim to provide a more rounded assessment of need.

Combining methodologies

The methodology described by Percy-Smith and Sanderson (1992) for their study of the health and welfare needs of a community in Leeds has the advantage of being grounded in the theory of human need developed by Doyal and Gough (1991). This takes as its starting point that there are basic human needs defined as 'universal pre-requisites for successful and, if necessary, critical participation in a social form of life' and summarized as 'physical health and autonomy' (Percy-Smith and Sanderson 1992: 8). The fulfilment of these basic needs requires that certain 'intermediate needs' – ranging from adequate nutritional food and water to a basic education – be met. For this to happen, there are 'specific satisfiers' or 'societal preconditions' which also need to be fulfilled. These are 'universal preconditions' – production, reproduction, cultural transmission and political authority – and 'preconditions for optimization' – negative and positive freedom, and political participation. The task of a needs audit, then, is to 'measure the levels at which all these intermediate needs are satisfied' and to 'identify those specific satisfiers which best meet local needs [specific goods, services and policies] and to monitor people's access to these' (Percy-Smith and Sanderson 1992: 11).

The authors argue that traditionally, there have been two opposing approaches to the assessment of need. On the one hand there is the top-down approach of 'experts' which seeks to measure need objectively and on the other, the 'bottom-up' approach which addresses itself to the subjective needs of people. The needs audit methodology aims to combine these approaches and, where they result in conflicting versions of need, to reconcile such differences. The methods employed in the study have all been described in this chapter. Analysis of existing information was used to obtain the 'objective' information favoured by experts. A postal survey of residents and follow-up with in-depth interviews with a subsample of these were used to identify the 'felt' needs of members of the community. Focus groups were convened with local voluntary and community groups and elected representatives to obtain a collective picture of needs and with local service providers to obtain the professionals' perspective. Finally, public meetings were organized at which conflicting versions of need could be set out and a process of negotiation begun (Percy-Smith and Sanderson 1992: 12–22).

Although not so theoretically driven, needs assessments in the public sector are beginning to involve a similar combination of methods. The discussion paper (NHS Management Executive 1991b) cited earlier in this chapter with reference to the epidemiological approach to health needs assessment also recommends comparative and corporate approaches. The first involves the use of secondary data to compare levels of service received and health outcomes in different areas. The corporate approach is designed to get different perspectives on health from clients, local people, and other local agencies as well as health professionals. In a related paper surveys and interagency discussions are cited as possible methods of obtaining this information (NHS Management Executive 1991a).

Housing needs assessments may also combine data collection methods. *A Guide to Local Housing Needs Assessment*, published by the Institute of Housing, recommends the use of housing need surveys in conjunction with wide ranging analyses of secondary data to provide a 'comprehensive and comprehensible picture of the local housing situation' (Van Zijl 1993: 119). Finally, in relation to training needs, guidelines produced for the Training and Enterprise Councils for England and Wales also describe a range of methods for obtaining information on needs as they apply to local labour markets (Employment Department 1992).

These approaches are perhaps more eclectic, or even opportunistic, than rounded but at least they involve an implicit recognition of the complex character of need. It is because of this complexity that methodologies for needs assessment need to include diverse but complementary methods.

Conclusion

In this chapter a range of different methods have been examined that can and have been used in needs assessment. These include methods which rely principally on the collation and analysis of existing (secondary) information, including social indicators, and those which are more concerned with the collection and analysis of new (primary) information. Both approaches have their uses depending on the purpose behind the needs assessment, the resources available and the conceptualization of need that is being deployed. However an over-reliance on secondary data alone can result in difficulties because the data may not have been originally collected for the purpose of assessing need. This can result in practical difficulties in terms of analysing and making effective use of data, and more fundamental objections since existing information is likely to reflect existing policy and professional priorities. As a result an assessment of need carried out on this basis may only result in a marginal change to existing provision rather than a more fundamental review. As a result the approach to needs assessment advocated here seeks to capitalize on the positive elements of a number of different approaches and methods – quantitative and qualitative, involving both existing and new data – in order to provide a fuller picture.

References

Cresswell, T. (1992) Unemployment and health: The development of the use of PRA in identified communities in Staveley, north Derbyshire, *RRA Notes*, Special Issue on Applications for Health, 16: 27–30.

Department of the Environment (DoE) (1994) *Index of Local Conditions*. London: HMSO.

Department of Health (1991) *Care Management and Assessment: Practitioner's Guide*. London: HMSO.

Doyal, L. and Gough, I. (1991) *A Theory of Human Need*. London: Macmillan.

Dun, R. (1989) *Pictures of Health?* London: West Lambeth Health Authority Community Services Unit.

Employment Department (1992) *Training and Enterprise: Developing Good Practice; Conducting a Skills Audit*. Sheffield: Employment Department.

Hawtin, M., Hughes, G. and Percy-Smith, J. (1994) *Community Profiling: Auditing Social Needs*. Buckingham: Open University Press.

IFF Research Ltd (1993) *Skill Needs in Britain – 1993*. London: IFF Research Ltd.

Jarman, B. (1983) Identification of underprivileged areas, *British Medical Journal*, 286: 1705–9.

Knox, A. and Chapman, P. (1995) Your health – Your say, *Cities*, 12 (2): 111–14.

London Borough of Southwark (1987) *Fair Shares? The Southwark Poverty Profile*. London: Southwark Planning.

Midwinter, A. and Monaghan, C. (1990) *The Measurement and Analysis of Rural Deprivation*. Glasgow: University of Strathclyde.

Mitra, A. (1994) Use of focus groups in the design of recreation needs assessment questionnaires, *Evaluation and Programme Planning*, 17 (2): 133–40.

Newham Youth Services (1994) *A Statistical Profile of Young People aged 11–21*. London: London Borough of Newham.

NHS Management Executive (1991a) *Moving Forward – Needs, Services and Contracts*. London: Department of Health.

NHS Management Executive (1991b) *Assessing Health Care Needs*. London: Department of Health.

Percy-Smith, J. and Sanderson, I. (1992) *Understanding Local Needs*. London: Institute for Public Policy Research.

Policy Research Unit (1993) *People, Jobs and Training in Wirral City Lands Volume 1*. Leeds: Policy Research Unit.

Policy Research Unit (1994) *Sandford Community Needs Project – Final Report*. Leeds: Policy Research Unit.

Reeve, D. (1991) *The Kirklees Social Needs Map: An Analysis of Community Charge and Rebate Data*. Huddersfield: Centre for Local and Regional Analysis, Huddersfield Polytechnic.

Richards, S. (1994) Making sense of needs assessment, *Research, Policy and Planning*, 12 (1): 5–9.

Theis, J. and Grady, H.M. (1991) *Participatory Rapid Appraisal for Community Development*. London: International Institute for Environment and Development.

Van Zijl, V. (1993) *A Guide to Local Housing Needs Assessment*. Coventry: Institute of Housing.

Wainwright, D. (1994) On the waterfront, *Health Service Journal*, 104: 28–9.

PART II

NEEDS ASSESSMENT
IN PRACTICE

4

MARTIN BROWNE

NEEDS ASSESSMENT AND COMMUNITY CARE

Introduction

The NHS and Community Care Act 1990 came into effect on 1 April 1993 and heralded a new era in the delivery of social care. Lead responsibility for community care was placed in the hands of local authority social services departments. This entailed assessing the needs of individuals and populations and enabling, but not necessarily providing, the flexible delivery of services sensitive to people's needs.

This chapter examines the policies and strategies that aim to transform social care for older people and people with physical disabilities, mental health problems, learning disabilities, drug or alcohol problems, or HIV/AIDS from a service-led to a needs-led system. First, the historical background and the policy context for the changes are set out. Then the methodologies adopted for the assessment of needs of both individuals and populations are described. Next, a number of issues that have emerged as a result of the adoption of a needs-led approach to service delivery are discussed. Finally, needs assessment is considered in terms of the impact on service users and joint working between agencies.

Historical background

The term 'community care' first appeared in an official report in 1929 (Wistow *et al.* 1994: 3) and its meaning has been debated ever since. However the origins of the current community care policy are far more recent. Although elements of the policy can be found in the 1968 Seebohm report (Wistow *et al.* 1994) it is the developments since 1985 that have been of most significance in shaping the current policy. It took three reports, one White Paper, the NHS and

Community Care Act 1990 and eight years to develop the community care policy that is currently in place.

In 1985 the House of Commons Social Services Select Committee produced its report *Community Care*. This was followed in 1986 by the Audit Commission's *Making A Reality of Community Care*. Taken together these two reports had a major impact on social policy: 'the Social Services Committee ... was instrumental in placing community care on the policy agenda ... the Audit Commission ... ensured that it has remained there ever since' (Wistow *et al.* 1994: 3).

The Audit Commission's report in particular was critical about community care, alleging that the policy was at best problematic and at worst contradictory. Concern was expressed about a number of issues including the way in which the social security system of payments for residential and nursing homes distorted the outcomes for people needing social care; the confusion over different agencies' responsibilities; and the disincentives to local authorities to invest in community care (Wistow *et al.* 1994: 3). The Commission concluded that the government had to respond or else there would be 'a continued waste of resources and, worse still, care and support that is either lacking entirely or inappropriate to the needs of some of the most disadvantaged members of society' (Audit Commission 1986: 5).

The government's response was to call in Sir Roy Griffiths whose previous damning report on the health service led to far-reaching changes in the management and organization of the NHS (Griffiths 1983). His report on community care, *Agenda For Action* (1988), was no less damning, but it was far less well received by ministers. In Griffiths's view there could be few areas where 'the gap between political rhetoric and policy on the one hand, or policy and reality in the field have been so great' (Griffiths 1988: iv). The system created 'perverse incentives' (Wistow *et al.* 1994: 6) to place people in residential and nursing homes, the costs of which were contributing to an ever-increasing social security budget. Griffiths's solution was to place responsibility for funding community care in the hands of social services departments by means of a specific budget, a solution which went against the grain of all previous government policy towards local government. Throughout the 1980s the government had systematically restricted local authority budgets and their control over the local delivery of services and to their dismay *Agenda For Action* was recommending a reversal of that policy. For this reason the government's response to Griffiths was a long time coming.

Agenda For Action was published in March 1988. However it was not until July 1989 that Kenneth Clarke, then Secretary of State for Health, responded to the report by means of a parliamentary statement. This heralded the publication in December 1989 of the White Paper, *Caring For People: Community Care in the Next Decade and Beyond*. The changes proposed in it were intended to 'promote choice and independence' (Secretaries of State 1989: para. 1.8) through 'services that respond flexibly and sensitively to the needs of individuals and carers ... that intervene no more than is necessary to foster independence; [and] ... that concentrate on those with the greatest needs' (para. 1.10).

Caring For People set out six key objectives:

- to promote domiciliary, day and respite services to enable people to live in their own homes;
- to ensure that service providers make practical support for carers a high priority;
- to promote the development of the independent sector alongside public services;
- to clarify agencies' responsibilities;
- to introduce a new funding structure;
- to make proper assessment of need and good case management the cornerstone of high quality care.

(para. 1.11)

There were seven key changes proposed in *Caring For People:*

- Local authorities were to become the lead agencies for community care.
- Local authorities would have to publish community care plans.
- Maximum use would have to be made of the independent sector.
- A new funding structure for those seeking public support for residential and nursing home care would be established, giving local authorities responsibility for the financial support of these people.
- Eligibility for income support and housing benefit would be the same whether people were in their own homes or in independent residential or nursing homes.
- Local authorities would have to establish inspection and registration units to check independent sector residential homes and their own homes.
- A new specific grant would be introduced to promote the development of social care for seriously mentally ill people.

(para. 1.12)

The White Paper became the NHS and Community Care Act on 29 June 1990. However, implementation was phased in over three stages from April 1991 to April 1993 in order to hold down community charge levels (Wistow *et al.* 1994: 11).

Policy context

There are several underlying themes which have determined the shape of community care policy in the 1990s. First, there is the steady growth in the numbers of elderly people in Britain. In 1991 there were around 8.8 million people over the age of 65 and more than 10 million above pensionable age (Meredith 1993: 19). Between 1990 and 2000 the number of people aged over 85 years is expected to grow by 35 per cent to well over one million people (Livesley and Crown 1992: 10,19). Although old age is not an illness it does lead to an increased likelihood of ill health and need for care.

Second, during the 1980s the cost of providing residential and nursing home care spiralled upwards. Unlike health and local authority budgets, the budget in the hands of the Department of Health and Social Security which provided funds to individuals being cared for in residential and nursing homes was not cash limited. Between 1979 and 1991 the amount of money claimed to support individuals in residential and nursing homes grew from £10 million to £1872 million and the number of claimants grew from 12,000 to 231,000 (Wistow *et al.* 1994: 6).

Third, a dominant theme in government policy during the 1980s and 1990s has been a drive towards the 'marketization' of public services. In the name of efficiency and effectiveness, services that had previously been directly provided by local authorities, health authorities and the civil service were hived off and either put out to tender to the highest bidder or established as separate agencies. Examples of this include the NHS internal market which established the purchaser/provider split between health authorities and hospital trusts and the creation of GP fundholders; and the concept of the enabling local authority which has seen services like housing management, refuse collection and ground maintenance put out to compulsory competitive tendering.

The fourth theme was the development of the consumerist model of public services which sought to turn the population of a local authority area and in particular, users of local government services into customers with means of redress through, for example, the Citizen's Charter. Such policies have given citizens more information about the work of local authorities and greater freedom of choice, but it is debatable whether people are really empowered through such measures.

Finally, and more specifically related to health and social care, was the idea of interagency collaboration and working in order to make the most effective use of limited resources. The reports of the Audit Commission, the Social Services Select Committee and Sir Roy Griffiths all refer to the need to improve interagency collaboration as did other reports that appeared at the same time. This was identified as needing to take place at both a strategic and an operational level.

Having set out the background to the community care changes and the context in which these changes should be seen, the following section describes what needs assessment means in practice for those affected by community care.

Methodology

Individual needs assessment

As a result of the community care changes enacted in April 1993, local authorities have a duty to 'assess people's needs holistically in relation to a wide range of possible service options, rather than having separate service-led assessments' (Department of Health 1991a: 4). This is a significant change of ethos for social services departments. People are no longer to be fitted into existing services, but services are to be built around individualized need. Thus someone presenting themselves to the department would not be assessed in terms of their eligibility for a particular service, but in terms of their needs, and the associated causes, so that a package of care, or 'care plan' can be built around them. Assessment of need is a key step in the wider process known as care management. This starts with an enquiry by a member of the public and then moves through screening and referral to the assessment. The assessment is followed by care planning and implementation of the care plan, which in turn is monitored and subsequently reviewed.

Caring For People states that the aim of assessment 'should be first to review the possibility of enabling the individual to continue to live at home ... and if that possibility does not exist, to consider whether residential or nursing home care would be appropriate' (Secretaries of State 1989: para. 3.2.3). The key attributes of the assessment process are that it should be widely publicized; needs-based; should take account of the wishes of the individual and their carers; collaborative; cost-effective; and have outcomes related to the stated objectives and priorities of the local authority (Department of Health 1991a: 39).

In 1991 the Department of Health issued its good practice guidance on *Care Management and Assessment* (1991b, 1991c) to those affected by the community care changes contained in the NHS and Community Care Act 1990. This guidance describes in detail the changes required of local authorities to implement community care successfully: changes in organization, practice and policy. *The Practitioner's Guide* (Department of Health 1991c) explained the sequence of events necessary for an assessment of need:

1 *Negotiate scope of assessment*: The assessment of need 'should be as simple, speedy and informal as possible ... based on the principle of what is the least that it is necessary to know to understand the needs being presented [and] to justify the investment of public resources' (para. 3.3). The scope of the assessment has to be negotiated between the assessing practitioner and the user in order that 'the individual's needs are to be seen in their proper social context' (para. 3.5). Decisions are also made as to whether other people or other care agencies need to be involved. The effective use of resources is a key issue: 'the assessment input should be commensurate with the likely input of care resources or the likely saving on resources' (para. 3.7).

2 *Choose setting*: The location of the assessment has to be decided by the assessing practitioner. It may be cheaper to conduct the assessment in the office, but if the assessment is concerned with maintaining the individual in their own home then it is more appropriately carried out in that setting.

3 *Clarify expectations*: Practitioners must ensure that users understand what the procedure involves, the timescale, the possible outcomes, the user's entitlement to information, participation, representation and their right to withdraw at any stage. The guidance assumes that people will be used to the service-led approach and that practitioners will need to educate them to the possibilities of a needs-led system.

4 *Promote participation*: The potential user needs to be actively involved in the process, as far as this is possible, which requires that the practitioner identifies 'the strengths as well as the weaknesses of an individual' (para. 3.21).

5 *Establish relationship of trust*: This is seen as important if the process is to truly reflect the needs of the individual.

6 *Assess need*: Self-assessment is the starting point of the needs assessment: 'the assessment should normally be guided by what the potential user volunteers as the presenting problem, only probing further with the individual's consent' (para. 3.33). The guidance goes on to suggest that a consensus should be sought between the practitioner, the user, the carer and any other care agencies involved, although 'the user's views should carry the most weight' (para. 3.34). Ultimately, power lies in the hands of practitioners since they are responsible for the final definition of users' needs. As well as defining need the assessor has to identify as precisely as possible the causes of the needs since 'the proper identification of the cause is the basis for selecting the appropriate service response' (para. 3.32).

7 *Determine eligibility*: Local authorities have to define in policy statements the types of need that warrant intervention. This then allows the practitioner to decide on the eligibility of users for assistance.

8 *Set priorities*: Within the assessment process the practitioner and user agree the relative priorities of the needs for which assistance is available. These have to be matched against the priorities of the agency or authority which, as with eligibility criteria, should be spelled out in policy statements.

9 *Agree objectives*: The final stage in the assessment is to agree the objectives for each of the prioritized needs in order that they can be monitored and reviewed: 'objective setting is . . . the key to effective care management' (para. 3.51).

10 *Record the assessment*: The assessment is recorded on a pro forma which can, if appropriate, be filled in by the user. The user should normally be given a copy of the assessment of needs.

(quotations from Department of Health 1991c)

The key stage in this process is obviously stage six, assessing need. The practice guidance indicates that agencies are at liberty to determine their own levels of assessment, according to policies, priorities and personnel, but six levels of assessment can be distinguished. These range from a 'simple' assessment for people with a simple need that can be met by a single agency, for example a bus pass; through a 'limited' assessment for low-risk needs which still require a single agency response, for example low level domiciliary support; to a 'comprehensive' assessment where a person's needs are multiple, interrelated and high-risk and will require a multi-agency response. Different local authorities have adopted different assessment frameworks and/or different terminology. Along with varying eligibility criteria and differing priorities, this hinders effective comparisons of service activity between districts.

The comprehensive assessment, as its name implies, collects the most information about a person's circumstances and needs. The Department of Health (1991c) suggests the sort of information such an assessment should collect. Having ascertained the person's biographical details, the assessment should start with a person's own perception of their needs. Then, a person's ability to perform various self-care activities should be assessed, along with physical and mental health indicators. The assessment should take into account the needs of carers: the care they provide; their relationship to the potential user; their expressed needs for support; their own physical and mental health and emotional state; their other commitments; and their future capacity. Information should be collected on a person's social networks and other sources of support. An assessment should ascertain what other care services a person is receiving and what their housing and transport needs are. Central to the assessment should be an evaluation of risk. Finally, the finances of the potential user and carer are looked at to see whether they are claiming all the benefits to which they are entitled. With regards to financial support from the local authority with fees for residential or nursing homes only the user's finances are subject to means-testing.

Caring For People and the guidance documents encourage authorities to keep assessments as simple as possible on the grounds of resource constraints and trusting users' assessments of their needs:

> The professional argument that a more comprehensive assessment may be justified on the grounds that it may uncover other needs, loses weight in the context of departments struggling to meet even presenting needs. It is further diminished by the new emphasis on trusting in the judgement of users and carers about their own needs
>
> (Department of Health 1991a: 45)

Population needs assessment

Community care is not only concerned with individual assessment of need. The White Paper, *Caring For People*, when describing the nature and contents of local authority community care plans stated that 'social services authorities will be expected to set out their assessment of the needs of the population they serve' (Secretaries of State 1989: para. 5.10). For good reasons, far less attention has been paid to population needs assessment in the context of community care than to individual needs assessment. In fact the Department of Health only issued its good practice guidance on population needs assessment (Department of Health 1993) three months before implementation and after the first community care plans were published. The fact that population needs assessment has been overshadowed by the individual needs assessment has resulted in far less developed methodologies: 'Assessing population needs is a massive new task for local authorities, who have had limited time and resources with which to complete it' (Stalker 1994: 8).

The Department of Health, through its practice guidance, has sought to encourage social services departments to 'plan and implement community care strategies on a sound base of information about local populations' (Department of Health 1993: 2). A 'pragmatic' definition of need is provided as the starting point, namely 'the ability of an individual or collection of individuals to benefit from care' (Department of Health 1993: 6). The guidance stresses that the purpose of population needs assessment is to provide an information base for strategic planning, but not to define the strategies for meeting those needs.

Population needs assessment is a dynamic and iterative process which involves four key stages. The first stage is to build up a population profile based on a range of data that can be both quantitative and qualitative. To carry out primary research for this purpose alone would clearly be an expensive and time-consuming operation. Blackman (1995) outlines a variety of existing sources of information. First, the national Census of Population conducted every 10 years provides information at a small area level. Unfortunately, this information becomes less accurate in the years following the Census. This may be a particular problem in urban areas where the population can change quite rapidly. Other sources, such as enhanced electoral registration population surveys or Family Health Service Authority age/sex registers, can help to overcome these deficiencies. Second, to estimate the needs of particular groups, such as people with physical disabilities, national prevalence data can be applied to the local population figures. One major source of prevalence data is the national disability surveys conducted by the Office of Population Censuses and Surveys. Applying national data to the local population in this way has to be done with caution. Not only can there be problems regarding definitions of disability, but also it does not account for local factors such as deprivation. To overcome this Blackman (1995) suggests comparing the prevalence rates with client information and local surveys. As community care progresses it should also be possible to include data from individual needs assessments to enhance the profile.

The second stage in the process combines the population profile with the development and implementation of strategic plans. The profile is seen as one element of the strategic planning process which also takes into account legislation and policy guidance, local values, national and local resource utilization, quality standards, budget and resources. The strategic planning process should define relative levels of need, priorities and preferred care package options. This in turn 'provides a framework for individual assessment and care management ... at the operational level' (Department of Health 1993: 20) with the aim of ensuring departmental consistency. If the social services department costs 'typical' care packages for different client groups and levels of need it can then model these against the population profile to estimate the service provision required and the budget implications: 'If this exceeds the budget available, further prioritisation has to be carried out by raising the threshold of need necessary to qualify for services or amending the care packages to reduce their cost' (Blackman 1995: 178). The aim of costing care packages, modelling the budget and projecting need is 'to plan expenditure by basing budgets on actual types and level of need' (Blackman 1995: 178).

The third stage is the use of individual needs assessment alongside population needs assessment. The aim is to refine profiles by utilizing the information that emerges from individual assessments and care plans, carers' and users' views, health authorities and individuals' care histories. Recording systems should be consistent with the presentation of population needs assessment information and should collect 'information on presented needs which are not subsequently addressed in care packages' (Department of Health 1993: 24), in other words unmet need. Although many departments have been reluctant to collect this information, it is seen as vital in the process of reviewing strategic plans.

The outcome measures that emerge from stage three – such as assessed needs of individuals, care packages provided and the effectiveness of those care packages – inform the fourth stage of the process, the review of the strategic plan. The extent to which outcomes can be measured is in no small part related to the quality of the recording procedures for individual needs assessments. One of the key elements of the assessment of individual needs is the pro formas used by departments from referral to review. Designing these pro formas creates tensions at both the practitioner and the policy level between the time taken to complete a form and enter the data on a computer and the amount of information required to make an accurate assessment of an individual's needs and to project needs for the population as a whole.

> Good results will follow from practitioners recording good quality information which makes limited demands on their time and the assessment [and] from significant investment in information systems which capture key data economically at all stages from referral to review.
> (Blackman and Stephenson 1995: 27)

Since the assessment of population needs is seen as a cyclical process this process of review should then feed back into the original population profile.

So although in theory needs assessment for community care is conducted at two levels utilizing different methodologies, in practice these two levels are not separate, but closely interdependent and intertwined. As such the following discussion of the issues related to needs assessment and community care considers both sides of the equation, individual and population, simultaneously.

Issues

The implementation of the community care changes and the subsequent development of needs assessment for individuals and for planning purposes has raised a number of practical and theoretical issues:

- what is need and who defines it?
- to what extent is the system now needs-led?
- unmet need;
- the link between population needs and individual needs;
- assessment as a tool for rationing;
- the boundary between social care and health care.

The first issue that has faced local authorities, practitioners and users has been what is meant by 'need' in the context of community care. Apart from stating that need is dynamic, relative and multifaceted the White Paper, the NHS and Community Care Act 1990 and the practice guidance do not set a common or an unequivocal definition of need. Doyal (1993: 276) argues that 'the absence of a clear and detailed theory of human need on which accurate needs assessment can be based' is an obstacle 'that jeopardises the potential success of the new policies'. The expectation is that through the twin approaches of assessment at the user level and population profiles at the policy level a commonly understood definition will emerge:

> The main purpose of the [community care] changes is to put needs of users and their carers at the centre. To this end authorities must introduce assessment procedures at the operational level, and set priorities at the strategic level which translate into eligibility criteria.
>
> (Audit Commission 1993: 3)

The summary of the practice guidance starts by saying that 'it is essential that all care agencies and practitioners share a common understanding of the term "need"' (Department of Health 1991c: 12). It goes on to suggest that the term is

> a shorthand for the requirements of individuals to enable them to achieve, maintain or restore an acceptable level of social independence or quality of life, as defined by the particular care agency or authority ... Need is a dynamic concept, the definition of which will vary over time in accordance with changes in national legislation, changes in local policy, the availability of resources [and] the patterns of local demand. Need is thus a relative concept ... to be defined at the local level.
>
> (Department of Health 1991c: 12)

Thus responsibility for defining need rests on local agencies and local assessors. It is up to local authority members to define need, to publicize this definition and to ensure that 'they are able to resource the response to the needs for which they accept any responsibility' (Department of Health 1991c: 12). Along with the fact that at the micro level practitioners are ultimately responsible for defining users' needs, what we have here is a concept of need that ultimately is the expert view, albeit with an element of user consultation. However, it is extremely unlikely that a centrally determined definition of need will be forthcoming since this would require the government to be explicit about the needs worthy of service intervention. Leaving the definition in the hands of local policy makers absolves the government of any responsibility for social care and is intended to ensure that blame, should it arise, is focused at the town hall, not the government front bench.

The second issue is the extent to which community care is needs-led rather than service-led. Although it may be the case that individual needs assessment should rely upon a locally-determined definition of need, the problem this creates is that agencies have *carte blanche* to deliver widely differing services. What qualifies as a need requiring a response in one district may not in another, thus undermining any notion of universality in this area of welfare provision. Furthermore the definition of need embodied in the policies of the local authority is set with resources very much in mind, resources that are centrally determined and historically demand-led.[1] So it could be argued, at least from the user's view, that the extent to which the delivery of social care services now differs from before April 1993 is negligible since resources, policy and professionalism are still the key determinants in the outcome of an assessment of needs. Richards (1994: 6) suggests that the operationalization of need by the same agency responsible for delivering services undermines the argument that there is a distinction between community care's needs-led approach and the previous service-led approach. The difference between service-led and needs-led assessment is that 'instead of having to conform to service eligibility criteria, the assessed needs of service users must conform to the agency's definition of eligible need if services are to be provided' (Richards 1994: 6). In other words, if services are to be truly needs-led the assessor must be separate from the agency setting the definitions of need, eligibility and priorities.

The third issue is that of unmet need. Local authority members are responsible for making and publicizing policy statements which define needs for their area, the level of priority of these needs and the eligibility criteria for a particular service response. At the individual level the practitioner defines need for the individual in relation to these policy statements. The guidance says that:

> This definition of needs should be incorporated into publicity material which clearly distinguishes between needs that are a mandatory, legislative responsibility and those that are a discretionary duty under the law, assumed as a matter of local policy.
>
> (Department of Health 1991c: 12)

Reference is not made to unmet need, but to shortfalls in service which when identified during assessment 'are a particularly important source of bottom-up information, and should be recorded systematically for planning purposes'. Shortfalls can occur in two ways. First, the needs of a person may not meet an authority's eligibility criteria. Second, a person can qualify under the criteria for a service that can be provided under a power rather than a duty, but the resources are insufficient to meet the need fully or partly (Audit Commission 1993: 4). The problem is related to the lack of a common statutory definition of need and the corresponding national diversity in the system. If there is no service response because of resource constraints then a person could argue that at another time in the same place they would have received a service. Likewise if service does not occur as a result of a failure to meet the eligibility criteria of that authority then a person could argue that at the same time in another place their self-same need would have qualified for a service response. These fears have made practitioners cautious about the extent to which they record service shortfall which in turn affects the quality of information available for service planning. The question is 'whether unmet need should be recorded in respect of individual assessments or simply aggregated en masse' (Stalker 1994: 5). Since the former approach would allow users to access this information and thus raise the spectre of judicial review, authorities have been reluctant to record the information at all.

The fourth issue that arises concerns the extent to which local authorities are making the link between individual and population needs assessment. From the practical view there is a question mark over the quality of information and information systems. The Audit Commission (1994: 6–7) has recorded that nearly all authorities have made estimates of needs for all client groups, although most are 'partial' and based on incomplete information. In particular the systematic recording of information and the use of information from practitioners and care managers has been limited. Stalker (1994: 5–6) argues that this is due to the lack of sophisticated information systems and the running down of information and planning sections by social services departments in the 1980s. Blackman and Stephenson (1995: 26) indicate that 'progress is needed . . . to link more closely individual assessment of clients with strategic planning'. A second, and more theoretical, issue regarding the relationship between population and individual needs assessments emerges from the practice guidance on the former (Department of Health 1993). The model proposed by the Department of Health states that the strategic plans that set the framework for individual needs assessment should draw on population profiles that use information from individual needs assessments. Is there not therefore an element of self-fulfilling prophecy here? If the strategic plan frames the individual assessment and the individual assessment informs the strategic plan then there is a risk that the need eligible for service is simply the need receiving service: what is being identified as need is actually historical service data. Once again the issue is the extent to which the new community care system can be said to be truly needs-led.

The fifth issue related to needs assessment is the extent to which assessment is being used as a mechanism for the rationing of scarce welfare resources and constraining the emergence of an accurate picture of social need. One of the main forces for the community care reform was the spiralling cost of providing residential and nursing home care. The Special Transitional Grant (the money being transferred in stages from the Department of Social Security) is cash-limited and eventually will become part of local authorities' base budgets. Thus, unlike before, there are limits on the resources available to fund social care. Meredith (1993: 80) argues that needs assessment is being used as a smokescreen to hide the impact of these changes and to ration the resources. Since both the practitioner and the policy maker are working with a knowledge of agency resources then, whether consciously or unconsciously, needs assessment and policy statements can be seen as tools for rationing resources. Salter (1994) points out that health and local authorities can ration community care because they can influence both demand for and supply of services. The needs assessment process puts power into the hands of the assessor to determine demand whilst at the policy making level decisions are made about definitions of need, priorities and eligibility criteria which control supply. He argues that as resources are constrained further by central government the tendency will be to tighten the grip on both ends of the equation to balance the books:

> In order to ensure some match between the demand for community care and the resources available, health and local authorities will seek to maximise their individual powers over assessment and access mechanisms (demand control) and the supply of services.
>
> (Salter 1994: 130)

Many would argue that rationing these resources is neither necessary nor desirable and that all 'actual' social needs could be met if the policy were better funded. Also Meredith (1993) suggests that by rationing resources in this way the picture of need that emerges is not a true one, but one viewed through the myopia of resource decisions.

The final issue with regards to needs returns to the matter of definition, in this case at the boundary between social care and health care. Over the last 30 years health authorities have been reducing the number of continuing care beds that they provide for the elderly, mentally ill, mentally impaired and chronically sick (Dimond 1994). This is of great significance to users since services provided by the NHS are free at the point of delivery, but services provided by local authorities are subject to means-testing. Only in 1994 the health service commissioner ruled that Leeds Health Authority had been wrong to discharge a profoundly brain-damaged man to a nursing home at a cost of £6000 per year (Giles 1994; Pitkeathley 1994). The outcome of this was policy guidance that placed the responsibility for defining entitlement to continuing care at the door of local health authorities (Timmins and Waterhouse 1994). The problem facing both users and practitioners in different agencies contending with limited resources is the point at which need moves from the social to the health arena and vice versa. This will obviously be the subject of local negotiation over individual cases, but it is unlikely that users will have the final say even if their voices are heard. This failure to define explicitly what the differences are in practice between health care needs and social care needs will undoubtedly continue to vex all those with responsibility for caring for dependent people.

The impact on users and policy

There can be little doubt that the implementation of the community care changes in April 1993 has had a significant impact on the delivery of services for users, carers, practitioners and policy makers. The following section explores two of the themes promoted in *Caring For People*: user empowerment and joint working.

Empowerment of users and carers

An important theme underlying much of *Caring For People* (Secretaries of State 1989) was the idea of empowering users and carers. The White Paper allowed users and carers to have a say in the assessment of their needs (in some cases allowing them to complete the assessment pro formas themselves) and entitled them to a copy of the final assessment. Complaints procedures were also established for people to appeal against the outcome or any aspect of the process. Services should be flexible and offer choice to both users and carers. Meethan (1995: 133) describes the reforms as involving:

> Substantial changes in the pattern of power relations between service providers and service users [where] the users were no longer to be considered as passive recipients, but as active participants in the assessment of their needs.

There are two sides to the empowerment of users and carers. The first is the introduction of consumerism into community care services, bringing social care into line with other areas of Conservative public service policy. The practice guidance suggests that users and carers will be enabled 'to exercise the same power as consumers of other services' (Department of Health 1991b: 11). Thus the values of the market are imposed on the delivery of social care services. However, since assessors purchase care on behalf of users, and assessing agencies are simultaneously provider agencies 'in terms of product development purchasing power remains with the provider rather than the consumer' (Ellis 1993: 9). This said the individual's right to choose the services that best match their circumstances as they perceive them has been significantly strengthened. Users can challenge and overturn the service response decision made by a local authority, as was shown by the Hazell case in 1993.[2]

The second manner in which users and carers are empowered is by means of information. Although the assessment process does allow users and carers greater access to information than was the case previously, Ellis (1993: 9) argues that the problem is that the information still lies with the service providers and it is they who are responsible for educating service users to the potential of the new system. She compares the power given to users in the NHS and Community Care Act 1990 with the unimplemented Sections 1, 2 and 3 of the Disabled Persons Act 1986 and finds community care wanting. Where the Disabled Persons Act would have given users and carers the right to a written statement of needs identified in assessment and the response proposed, community care says users and carers should be informed of the result of assessment as a matter of good practice. Although most professionals would comply with good practice guidance, they may not always provide a written statement, particularly if there is not to be continuing service. The same comparison is made with the issue of advocacy. The Disabled Persons Act enabled people with disabilities to appoint an advocate to help put their case, whereas community care 'places the onus on the provider to facilitate understanding' (Ellis 1993: 10).

For one person's power to increase requires that someone else's power must diminish and those in positions of power are traditionally reluctant to let any of it slip away. Community care does empower users to a certain extent, but ultimately the professionals assessing needs and providing services still hold the purse strings and the reins. Meethan (1995: 143) suggests that those in power still have a lot to learn: 'The rhetoric of user choice and empowerment is one thing; in practice it needs to be matched by a corresponding unlearning of existing organisational and professional practices and hierarchies at all levels.'

Changes in policy and practice

One of the changes promoted in *Caring For People* was a new 'approach for achieving effective joint working, based on strengthened incentives and clearer responsibilities' (Secretaries of State 1989: para. 6.1). Although joint working and joint finance had been a feature of health and social care before the White Paper, one of the problems identified by Griffiths (1988) had been the confusion of responsibilities between agencies. Under the new arrangements social services departments are the gatekeepers to social care. Health authorities wishing to discharge patients to residential care have to work with local authorities to develop policies and strategies for achieving this. Effective arrangements need to be made for social work teams to conduct assessments in hospitals and to this end all local authorities have agreed arrangements for hospital discharge with health authorities (Audit Commission 1993: 6). Clinicians, community nurses and therapists need to be available for multidisciplinary assessments to take place. Thus policies and strategies need to be developed at a policy level between health and local authorities in order that arrangements can be made at the practice level. GPs are also called upon to contribute to assessments and local arrangements are promoted to facilitate GPs contribution to community care. Much of the research in this area suggests that joint working has not been problem-free. The issues have revolved around the practical problems of information and technology and the more fundamental differences in responsibility and accountability. On the first issue, in its report on the first year of community care, the Department of Health (1994: 4) stated that: 'Issues of technology, compatibility of information and confidentiality continue to impede a joint health/local authority approach to the collection and presentation of information about needs and provision.' However, the second issue is a more fundamental one. The question remains as to how much further joint planning can develop since local authorities and health authorities 'are accountable to different masters and subject, therefore, to differing demands and priorities' (Stalker 1994: 8). Ultimately, for as long as health and social care are administered by separate agencies, there will always be a line between their priorities, practices and budgets, not least because of the cash limits on both health and social care resources. In the words of Salter (1994: 130), 'whereas the formal change agenda requires agencies to dissolve barriers and act collaboratively, the informal rationing agenda . . . requires them to retrench, protect and husband their separate resources'.

Conclusion

The community care changes were never going to happen overnight; *Caring For People* acknowledges as much in its subtitle *Community Care in the Next Decade and Beyond*. The rapid change required of social services departments to implement community care successfully is part of a long term process designed to take social care into the next century. Undoubtedly, the biggest change has been the shift to needs-led systems of service delivery which has created problems at both the policy and the practice level for decision makers, assessors, users and carers which inevitably will take time to resolve.

At the policy level the Audit Commission's monitoring of community care suggests that social services departments need to develop more sophisticated ways of gathering and using information on needs to inform the planning process (Audit Commission 1994). Initially, population needs assessment came second to individual needs assessment in the implementation of community care, but now it needs to move centre stage, although this may require that departments review their whole strategic planning process. An investment of time and resources is required, to develop sophisticated information systems that can monitor and evaluate all stages of care management from initial referral through needs assessment to review. In particular, the issue of collecting information on unmet need has to be addressed if strategic planning is to project accurately potential demand.

On the operational side a number of pieces of research have highlighted the concerns of users and carers (Age Concern 1993; Audit Commission 1994; Johnson 1995). The major issue is the extent to which people feel informed about, and involved in, the assessment process. For example Johnson (1995: 3,4) reports an overreliance by practitioners on verbal rather than written forms of communication, users and carers being confused by comprehensive assessments and multiagency assessments militating 'against the full involvement of carers and, in particular, users'. The Audit Commission (1994: 8) reports similar problems ranging from difficulty finding out about services to feelings of exclusion from the whole process with little room for choice. Community care has the empowerment of users and carers at its heart, but these pieces of research suggest that there is still a long way to go if empowerment is going to turn from rhetoric to reality.

To replace a service-led system with a needs-led approach whilst simultaneously acquiring new budgetary responsibilities, different organizational structures and developing more collaborative ways of working has placed a tremendous strain on departments most of which, despite the inevitable difficulties, have coped with remarkably well. The latter part of a decade remains and the beyond beckons. It is still early days.

Notes

1 The Special Transitional Grant (STG), the budget to pay for community care, in 1993/94 totalled £565 million of which £399 million was the sum transferred from the Social Security budget. In other words almost 71 per cent of the budget was derived from the previous demand-led budget operated by the Department of Social Security. The 1993/94 STG was allocated to authorities partly on the basis of the Standard Spending Assessment (SSA) and partly according to the number of people already being supported by social security benefits in their areas. In 1994/95 it was allocated wholly on the basis of the SSA and the majority of the 1993/94 STG was transferred into authorities' base budgets. For further details see Audit Commission 1994.
2 In 1993 Mark Hazell, a young man with Down's syndrome, successfully challenged Avon Social Services Department's assessment of his needs and won the right to be placed in the long term placement of his choice. The case is described in detail in an article by Marchant (1993).

References

Age Concern (1993) *No Time to Lose: First Impressions of the Community Care Reforms.* London: Age Concern.
Audit Commission (1986) *Making a Reality of Community Care.* London: HMSO.
Audit Commission (1993) *Taking Care: Progress with Care in the Community.* London: HMSO.

Audit Commission (1994) *Taking Stock: Progress with Community Care*. London: HMSO.

Blackman, T. (1995) *Urban Policy in Practice*. London: Routledge.

Blackman, T. and Stephenson, C. (1995) Economic assessment, *Community Care*, 16–22 March: 26–7.

Department of Health (1991a) *Assessment Systems and Community Care*, London: HMSO.

Department of Health (1991b) *Care Management and Assessment: Manager's Guide*. London: HMSO.

Department of Health (1991c) *Care Management and Assessment: Practitioner's Guide*. London: HMSO.

Department of Health (1993) *Implementing Community Care: Population Needs Assessment Good Practice Guidance*. London: Department of Health.

Department of Health (1994) *Implementing Caring For People: Impressions of the First Year*. London: Department of Health.

Dimond, B. (1994) How far can you go? *Health Service Journal*, 14 April: 24–5.

Doyal, L. (1993) Human need and the moral right to optimal community care. In J. Bornat, C. Pereira, D. Pilgrim and F. Williams (eds) *Community Care: A Reader*. London: Macmillan in association with Open University Press.

Ellis, K. (1993) *Squaring the Circle: User and Carer Participation in Needs Assessment*. York: Joseph Rowntree Foundation.

Giles, S. (1994) Why no one wants to bite the bullet, *Health Service Journal*, 10 March: 11.

Griffiths, R. (1983) *Report of the NHS Management Enquiry*. London: Department of Health and Social Security.

Griffiths, R. (1988) *Community Care: Agenda For Action*. London: HMSO.

House of Commons Social Services Committee (1985) *Community Care*, second report, session 1984–5, HC13. London: HMSO.

Johnson, L. (1995) *Getting the Message: Users' and Carers' Experiences of Community Care in Leeds*. Leeds: Community Health Council.

Livesley, B. and Crown, J. (eds) (1992) *Assessing the Needs of Elderly People: Report of a Workshop Held at the Department of Health*. London: Research For Ageing Trust.

Marchant, C. (1993) What comes first? *Community Care*, 15 July: 18–19.

Meethan, K.F. (1995) Empowerment and community care for older people. In N. Nelson and S. Wright (eds) *Power and Participatory Development*. London: Intermediate Technology Publications.

Meredith, B. (1993) *The Community Care Handbook: The New System Explained*. London: Age Concern.

Pitkeathley, J. (1994) Who should pay for long-term care? *The Health Summary*, 11 (3): 1.

Richards, S. (1994) Making sense of needs assessment, *Research, Policy and Planning*, 12(1): 5–9.

Salter, B. (1994) The politics of community care: social rights and welfare limits, *Policy and Politics*, 22(2): 119–31.

Secretaries of State (1989) *Caring For People: Community Care in the Next Decade and Beyond*. Cm 849, London: HMSO.

Stalker, K. (1994) The best laid plans . . . gang aft agley? Assessing population needs in Scotland, *Health and Social Care*, 2(1): 1–9.

Timmins, N. and Waterhouse, B. (1994) Cradle to grave NHS buried by government, *The Independent*, 13 August.

Wistow, G., Knapp, M., Hard, B. and Allen, C. (1994) *Social Care In A Mixed Economy*. Buckingham: Open University Press.

5

ANNE FOREMAN

HEALTH NEEDS ASSESSMENT

Introduction

Health needs assessment can contribute to policy making within the National Health Service (NHS) through the provision of information of relevance to the strategic planning process of district health authorities (DHAs). More specifically, needs assessment can help DHAs to understand the health needs of their population, identify service shortfalls, prioritize and reallocate resources and thus play a vital role in the planning, contracting and evaluation processes.

This chapter will briefly explain the context in which the NHS reforms occurred and their implications in terms of the purchaser–provider split and the assessment of health needs. It will also outline key issues raised by the White Paper *Health of the Nation* (Secretary of State for Health 1991), the *Patient's Charter* (Department of Health 1991) and *Local Voices* (NHS Management Executive 1992) which, as we will see, also have implications for the assessment of need. A definition of health needs assessment is provided, followed by a brief discussion of the impact of traditional epidemiological/ medical, economic and social perspectives on the concept of health needs. Next the approach to needs assessment proposed by the DHA Discussion Document *Assessing Health Care Needs* (NHS Management Executive 1991) is examined and compared with other approaches and methods including, the locality needs approach, the life cycle framework, rapid appraisal, a community development approach and priority search. Finally, the overall impact of needs assessment on the health service planning process is considered.

Context

The potential role of health needs assessment in service planning was brought into focus with the introduction of the NHS reforms. These reforms were prompted by a number of issues which were of increasing concern to the government, not the least being the NHS 'funding crisis' of 1987. The major objectives of the reforms were to improve local management, to make better use of resources and to provide a better deal for patients and service users. This led the government to question the appropriateness of existing patterns of resource allocation and the effectiveness of service provision, and highlighted the need for more accurate information upon which to base strategic decision making.

The first step taken by the government to resolve these problems was to create the purchaser–provider split, which gave responsibility for strategic management to the purchaser of services (i.e. DHAs) and operational responsibility to the provider (i.e. hospitals and trusts). By so doing the government aimed to allow DHAs to take a more independent view of provider interests and ensure that through the contracting process decision making on service priorities would be more explicit than in the past and would take into consideration both the views of the public and the cost effectiveness of services. Under the legislation the DHAs' key responsibilities were defined as:

- to assess the state of the health of the people they serve;
- to assess what needs to be done to improve health;
- to set priorities for those improvements;
- to purchase effective services to meet those needs . . .
- to assess the effect of policies and programmes against key criteria.

(Parish 1994: 142)

These reforms created a context in which health needs assessment could play a crucial role in health service planning, by providing DHAs with information upon which to build their strategies, draw up contract specifications and to evaluate how effectively needs were being met. This was reinforced by the NHS and Community Care Act 1990 which made it a statutory responsibility for DHAs to undertake needs assessment. Guidance on how to implement the required assessments was provided by the DHA Discussion Paper *Assessing Health Care Needs* (NHS Management Executive 1991). The NHS reforms included the publication of *The Health of the Nation* (Secretary of State for Health 1991), *The Patient's Charter* (Department of Health 1991), and finally *Local Voices* (NHS Management Executive 1992) which were also of importance to the process of health needs assessment.

Based upon the principles and approaches identified by the World Health Organization (WHO), *The Health of the Nation* raised a number of issues which would influence the way in which health needs assessment was implemented. These issues included a recognition of the existence of health inequalities and an acknowledgement of the variety of factors which influence the population's health, thereby highlighting the need for a multiagency approach to health needs assessment and the role of public participation in decision making. The theme of public involvement continued with the introduction of *The Patient's Charter*, which showed the government expected the NHS to become more 'consumer orientated', giving patients more information about service provision and the standard of care they can expect.

Finally, the publication of *Local Voices* in 1992 emphasized that 'to give people an effective voice in the shaping of health services locally will call for different approach from that employed in the past' (Layzell 1994: ɔt only did *Local Voices* promote the idea that the public's views sought in relation to needs assessment, but also to inform priority ɛrvice specification and the monitoring of provision.

.clude, the government had set in place reforms which would change the management process within the NHS, the purchaser–provider split and the call for the comprehensive assessment of need providing the tools for action. The next section explains the role, and gives a definition of, health needs assessment and introduces three perspectives on the concepts of health and health need, which will form the basis for a discussion of a number of different approaches to health needs assessment.

Approaches to health and health need

The purpose of a health needs assessment is not to solve health problems directly, but to provide information which will inform the provision of services (either strategically or via contract specification) so those services may themselves contribute to the health of the population. Pickin and St Leger (1993: 6) define health needs assessment as 'the process of exploring the relationship between health problems in a community and the resources available to address those problems in order to achieve a desired outcome'. However health needs assessment and the concepts of health and need which underpin it are complex and contestable. There are three distinctive perspectives on health and health need that must be addressed, as they form the basis for the main approaches to health needs assessment. They are the epidemiological/medical, economic and social concepts of health and health need.

First, we consider the epidemiological/medical approach, according to which health can be seen as the absence of disease and health need is defined in terms of the presence of disease in a population. Service utilization records are therefore used as one indicator of need, reflecting the government view that the public express their need for health care through their demand for existing services.

Second, the health economist, while accepting the epidemiological approach to health need, stresses that needs assessment and the allocation of services occurs in a context of scarce resources. Since not all needs can be met and as needs are necessarily relative, it should be possible to trade one need off against another (using cost benefit analysis for example) and represent the difference between the needs numerically, to aid priority setting. This, the health economist suggests, will ensure that resources are used in a way that results in the maximum benefit for the population as a whole. Thus if treatments are ineffective they should be stopped and all remaining treatments should be pursued only to the extent that costs remain less than benefits. The influence of the economic perspective is reflected in the government's definition of health need as 'the ability to benefit from health care' (NHS Management Executive 1991: 5).

The third approach is the social perspective which is based on the WHO's definition that 'health is a state of physical, mental and social wellbeing and not merely the absence of disease or infirmity' (Bradshaw 1994: 48). More specifically health is determined by the ability of a person or group to 'on the one hand realise their aspirations and satisfy needs and on the other hand, to change or cope with the environment' (Bradshaw 1994: 48). This draws attention to two key issues; that disease is only one aspect of understanding health need, other social and environmental factors must also be considered; and that the personal nature of the health experience must be accounted for if a full understanding of health need is to be achieved.

There is much to be learned from a comparison of these perspectives on health and health need. The epidemiological concept is dominated by the medical profession's narrow definition of need in terms of disease. This, Wilkin *et al.* (1992: 4) suggest, is because they 'prefer to define needs in terms of specific techniques within their sphere of competence'. However this focus upon the process of health care fails to take into account other factors which might influence the population's health.

By contrast, the social model focuses on the interaction between health and other aspects of an individual's social, economic and environmental situation. It takes account not only of the treatment of a disease, but also the outcomes of treatment (i.e. the quality of life and sense of well-being which should result from treatment), and offers a more positive, holistic approach to health. Also, rather than rely solely on the professional's definition of health need, this approach highlights the importance of the lay person's perception of their own health needs.

The government definition of health and health need emphasizes the role of existing services and the views of experts which again results in a limited understanding of need and, as a consequence, confines potential change to the modification of existing services. The social approach, on the other hand, by focusing on people not services, provides more scope for reform and encourages a wider view of health and health care. But epidemiologists and health economists would argue that the goals set by the social model are hopelessly ambitious in the context of present NHS capacity. A final contrast is that, while the epidemiological and social models would attempt to meet all the needs which fall within their respective definitions, the economic model effectively replaces needs with the more restricted concept of priorities. This, as we will see, throws up difficult questions about how priorities should be set and who should have access to health care.

This brief discussion has focused on the main approaches to health and health need. Next we will see how these approaches affect the way in which health needs assessments are conducted.

Approaches to health needs assessment

In this section the approach to health needs assessment recommended by the government in *Assessing Health Care Needs* (NHS Management Executive 1991) and the methods it implies, will be outlined. A critique of this technique will be followed by a discussion of alternative and complementary methods and approaches which have the potential to enhance the understanding of health needs.

The government's approach to health needs assessment

The government sees health needs assessments as a means of gathering information of relevance to the development of contract specifications. Thus needs assessment will not only contribute to DHAs' knowledge of the population's health needs, but also inform the contracting process and provide guidance on the allocation of resources within the NHS.

The technique proposed by the government and outlined below takes a 'hybrid' approach to needs assessment. It is based primarily on the traditional epidemiological method, but is strongly influenced by economic approaches and some aspects of the social model. The approach comprises the following elements:

1 a statement of the problem, usually a disease, in context;
2 an outline of its subcategories relevant to service delivery;
3 an estimate of the range of incidence and prevalence rates for the problem, and its subcategories;
4 a summary of the services available – both in terms of care and care settings;
5 a summary of the known effectiveness and cost-effectiveness of the services;
6 a derivation of a range of models of care from 3 and 5 above;
7 a view on outcome measures, targets, information requirements and research priorities.

(NHS Management Executive 1991: 6)

This approach, following the epidemiological model, attempts to 'measure the total amount of ill health in the community, categorised by disease' (Donaldson and Mooney 1991: 1529). Services which could be used to meet this need are highlighted and their effectiveness assessed. Both sets of data are combined in order to decide which services can meet the identified need in the most appropriate and cost-effective way. It was anticipated that DHAs would use this approach to assess needs 'condition by condition', using cost-effectiveness as a means of deciding between competing claims for resources.

The methods entailed by the government's approach rely largely on the collection of baseline data from secondary sources. This information is used:

• to determine the presence of disease using sources including mortality and morbidity data, disease registers, the General Household Survey, the Annual Health Survey, and The Annual Report of the Director of Public Health;
• to illustrate the context of the disease by employing demographic information from the census of population, OPCS population estimates and projections and deprivation indices;
• to provide data on services, i.e. service activity data, health service indicators, hospital utilization rates, waiting lists, the evaluation of clinical

outcomes, effectiveness bulletins and the Annual Report of the Director of Public Health.

The above sources can be supplemented by interviews with experts to utilize their knowledge of previous practice and current medical opinion and, where necessary, local surveys based on a particular group in the population or disease category.

The aim is to assess not only the needs of the population, but also the cost-effectiveness of the services provided. Thus the epidemiological and economic approaches are combined in an attempt to encourage the provision of services which most cost-effectively maximize the health of the population. Donaldson and Mooney (1991: 1529) claim that the only way to maximize benefits is 'by comparing health care interventions with each other in terms of health gains produced for resources spent', discarding ineffective treatments and only funding effective treatments as long as the costs remain less than the benefits. One method which has been used to assess the relative benefit of service provision is the Quality Adjusted Life Year (QALY). This provides a unit of measurement for assessing the relative effectiveness of various treatments for a health problem. 'Health improvements are measured in terms of life expectancy, adjusted according to changes in quality of life resulting from the use of health services' (Donaldson and Donaldson 1993: 31). This approach would assist the process of prioritization by giving 'more resources to treatments with a low cost per quality adjusted life year (QALY) than to those with a high marginal cost per QALY gained' (Donaldson and Mooney 1991: 1529). However, as will be seen, questions have been raised about the appropriateness of using the QALY as a basis for resource allocation.

Issues arising from the government approach

The definition of health and health need used in the government approach has been criticized for being too narrow and too focused on disease categories. This has a number of implications. It does not facilitate other ways of looking at epidemiological data, for example in terms of age, gender or the spatial dimensions of need. Furthermore, the principal method employed by this approach, the collection of secondary medical and hospital activity data, means it does not actively seek out other non-medical sources of information. The results of the health needs assessment will be similarly limited in scope. Hamilton-Kirkwood and Parry-Langdon (1993: 8–9) claim there are difficulties with the information upon which the NHS has historically based need, such as hospital activity data, morbidity and mortality, 'not only in terms of completeness, accuracy, and timeliness, but also validity'. In addition, the concentration on disease fails to take sufficient account of the impact of social, economic and environmental factors on health and the need for health care. This, Poppay and Williams (1994: 104) believe, suggests a need for more flexible methods of needs assessment.

Problems with this approach also arise because needs are only defined within the context of existing health services, i.e. solutions to health problems are only sought from within the resource pool of the NHS. This has a number of ramifications. It reduces the possibility of multiagency working and fails to recognize the fact that other agencies outside the NHS can contribute to meeting health needs and that communities have resources which could be developed to help tackle health problems. It perpetuates the status quo in terms of service provision and the dominance of the medical profession in the definition and treatment of health needs. This approach risks simply fitting people into services, i.e. it will establish the public's eligibility to use an existing service, rather than challenging medical experts and providing a service which actively considers the public's perception of need. As a result, because the definition of need is narrow, its response is limited and any change will be minimal, thus the NHS will continue to be service-led, rather than needs-led.

A further set of criticisms of the government's approach has focused on the elements derived from the economic approach. Ham and Spurgeon (1992: 19) claim that information on cost-effectiveness in the NHS is 'seriously incomplete'. The economic approach limits needs assessment to a purely 'technical exercise' within the present health service and thus ignores the contribution other services can make. Attempts to prioritize resource allocation throw up questions about the basis on which priorities should be set and who should decide who will benefit most from treatment. These questions introduce equity issues, that is, what is the government's objective, horizontal equity, defined as the 'equal treatment of individuals who are equal in relevant respects', or vertical equity, 'requiring the proportionately unequal treatment of individuals who are unequal in relevant respects'? (Ong 1993: 3). If this issue can be decided, the question arises should prioritization be based on equality or 'on achieving the most cost-effective maximum overall health outcome from these scarce resources' (Lightfoot 1995: 107). Only purchasers and policy makers can decide. Health is an emotive issue, no method can hope to be purely objective and value judgements are unavoidable in the assessment of health need. The only satisfactory basis upon which to make decisions is for the purchaser first to be aware of the value framework in which they work and then to ensure they have access to a wide range of data with which to inform the planning process.

Despite these criticisms epidemiological data, were it to be collected in a more systematic manner, could provide a baseline for the assessment of needs. Similarly the economic approach, by asserting the necessity for priority setting, could also contribute to the understanding of health need, but only once the ethical questions raised by its technical solutions are resolved. Both elements of the government's approach are constrained by the concepts underpinning them and could benefit from the broader insights into needs assessment offered by alternative methods.

Approaches to health needs assessment based on the social model

The government recognized the limitations of both the epidemiological/economic approach and the purchaser's present capability to undertake health needs assessments and therefore proposed a 'corporate' approach to needs assessment (NHS Management Executive 1991), which takes account of the views of other interested parties such as GPs, providers, local authorities and the public. This approach was not given a particularly high profile. However, the application of alternative approaches and methods is vital, first to overcome some of the problems with the approach to needs assessment outlined above, and second to contribute to a fuller understanding of the public's health needs. The approaches to be discussed include the locality needs approach, the life cycle framework, rapid appraisal, a community development approach and priority search. These entail the use of a number of social research methods including in-depth interviews, focus groups, surveys and public meetings.

The locality needs approach and life cycle framework

The epidemiological approach was criticized for basing its assessment purely on the presence of disease and failing to promote other ways of looking at epidemiological data. Alternative strategies are offered by the locality needs approach and the life cycle framework. The locality needs approach aims to promote more accurate targeting of resources by focusing on meeting the needs of populations in small areas. It divides the population into geographical groups which, for example, can be centred around GP practices or specific communities and relates epidemiological data to relevant demographic and social variables such as the number of elderly people or people suffering from a long term illness (for more details see Pickin and St Leger 1993).

The life cycle framework collects information on mortality and morbidity, health resources and service options, but analyses the data in a demographic context which recognizes the influence of age and gender on individual's experience of health and health care and asserts that unless they are taken into account neither services nor policies can accurately reflect the needs of the population (for more details see Pickin and St Leger 1993).

This framework also seeks to challenge the epidemiological approach by asserting that 'modifiers', such as socioeconomic, environmental, ethnic and cultural background, influence the health experience of a community. Therefore health need must be assessed in a broader context than that proposed by the government approach. The life cycle approach forms a contrast with the limitations of the epidemiological method by collecting data within a framework which 'does not force thinking to be constrained by what information currently happens to be available' (Pickin and St Leger 1993: 14). The framework is also flexible and accepts the possibility that the information it collects may readjust its understanding of the health needs and how they may be met. Finally, when the framework is used to assess the resources available to meet health needs, the researcher's perception is not dominated by health care or even statutory services (although these are accounted for), as the framework considers health in a broader context, first analysing the resources available within the individual, their family and community, before considering the input of the 'formal health services'.

Rapid appraisal

One method which has gained favour with a number of purchasing organiz-ations is rapid appraisal, which attempts to bring together the views of what the government termed the 'interested parties' in needs assessment (NHS Management Executive 1991). This method seeks to overcome the professional dominance of needs assessment perpetuated by the government's approach, by enabling the community and professionals to work together to develop a joint understanding of a community's health needs. This will form the basis for action plans creating a foundation for continuing collaboration between professionals and the public.

Rapid appraisal uses local people both to identify problems and to contribute to solutions. Although the research team is made up of professionals, it accepts the multifaceted nature of health need and thus adopts a multiagency approach. A research team might therefore include purchasers, providers, GPs and officers from various local government departments such as social services and housing.

This method applies a wide definition of health and acknowledges the influ-ence of socioeconomic and environmental factors. Thus it collects infor-mation on community capacity, socioecological factors, present service provision and the influence of national, regional and local policies. The methods used to collect the data include in-depth interviews with local people, observation of the area and analysis of health service and local authority records, complemented by the knowledge of the research team. This infor-mation is then collated, analysed and priorities derived by professionals and local people working together in workshops. Although a largely qualitative method, the process does not deny the need for 'hard' epidemiological data, which is integrated into the action planning phase. 'Together these form a very powerful baseline for assessing the impact of services on the improvement of the life and health of populations' (Ong 1993: 913).

Again, like the life cycle framework, rapid appraisal acknowledges that people themselves have the capacity to take action to tackle the health prob-lems in their area with the support of statutory services. Thus Ong (1991: 913) believes 'The role of the professionals has therefore shifted into enabling, rather than determining priorities and strategies.' It is the professionals' willingness to adapt their view of health and health needs in the light of the research findings and accept the validity of the social model of health which is crucial to the success of rapid appraisal.

Rapid appraisal illustrates that acceptance of the multifactorial nature of health requires, and benefits from, a multiagency approach to needs assess-ment, partnership between professional and community being at the heart of it. This approach reveals the benefits of a more needs-led approach to identi-fying the public's feelings and priorities with regard to health and health care.

Community-led health needs assessment

Rapid appraisal is an example of a professionally-led approach to needs assess-ment. However advocates of the community development approach question the extent to which the community guides the process. They suggest an alternative community-led approach, through which the community itself takes the initiative to address health needs in its area. Such an approach needs the support of professionals, but 'does not involve the professionals simply teaching volunteers how to think, or imposing their own interpretation on the experiences of local people' (Wainwright 1994: 29). It expects the professionals to be prepared to alter their opinions and relinquish power over the research process, by making 'the skills and resources necessary to identify the health need of the local population available to members of that community' (Wainwright 1994: 28).

A variety of methods can be employed, including community development through a community worker, recruitment and training of lay volunteers to become involved in planning and running of a project and a social survey of the community (which should ideally be analysed jointly with local people to derive priorities and an action plan). A community development approach can challenge present responses to health needs through the belief that 'the satisfaction of health needs relies upon intervention in social and economic relations, rather than simply re-configuring existing agencies' (Wainwright 1994: 29).

This approach also contributes to the debate on health needs assessment, highlighting issues around the multisectoral approach, public participation and the influence of the professions on the outputs from health assessments. In particular it requires that the skills to undertake needs assessment be given to the community, a radical departure from the epidemiological method, but one which may lead to a more accurate understanding of community health needs and capacities. It is strongly grounded in the concepts of the social model and is widely used by grass roots community groups, although its impact on the policy process can be limited unless it has allies among the 'experts'.

Issues and problems

The approaches and methods discussed above provide a useful counterbalance to the epidemiological/economic approach to health needs assessment. In particular the social model entails a holistic approach to health and health needs which, in turn, would require a multisectoral response. However the social model also raises issues relating to the role of citizens in determining their own health needs and the implications of such involvement for the professional dominance of the process of health needs assessment.

Economists have criticized the holistic view of health for being overambitious and resulting in too broad a definition of need, one the health services could never hope to respond to. However it could equally be argued that the epidemiological/economic approach is too narrow, concentrating on disease and cost-effectiveness and failing to fully acknowledge that 'the causes of a particular health problem or disease are often multi-factorial and, therefore, require co-ordinated and collaborative action by a variety of organisations, authorities and individuals to combat or prevent it' (Institute of Health

Services Management and Faculty of Public Medicine 1991: 5). As many of the determinants of health lie outside the health services remit, one cannot expect the health services to tackle these issues alone. Other groups and organizations can contribute to the understanding and meeting of health needs. To work together effectively, however, requires pooling of information to avoid duplication of effort and improved awareness of the work others are doing. Furthermore such an approach reflects people's own perception of health. As Ong has found

> they did not define health as a separate category, and many problems that were identified fell outside the traditional medical remit, yet were firmly at the centre of a multi-disciplinary and multi-agency public health approach.
>
> (Ong *et al.* 1991: 913–14)

Traditionally it has been the professional who has dominated the assessment of need 'as they "ratify" expressed needs by providing a service. Furthermore, they have been able to shape needs through their own research and development actions' (Ong and Humphris 1994: 63). Yet the social model and the approaches reviewed above stress the importance of involving the public in the definition and assessment of need and of challenging the professional understanding of need, which is often bounded by 'the limited perspective of their own area of expertise' (Southern Community Health Research Unit 1991: 12). Indeed, Dr Brian Mawhinney, the Minister for Health, advocated this view, when in a speech in 1994 he said

> Knowledge of people's perceptions, preferences and experience of health services is essential in assessing health needs and how to meet them. We must get away from the notion that health services can be designed for the community by 'experts' who define people's needs but ignore their wishes.
>
> (Mawhinney 1994: 12)

Community participation in the process of health needs assessment can result in challenges to current priorities and practices, identification of possible new solutions to problems and the facilitation of multiagency working. However there is a risk that public expectations are raised beyond the level that can be addressed. In addition, Whitting (1994: 9) notes that undertaking public participation does leave the provider with the task of deciding the extent to which the views of the public should be weighted against those of experts and epidemiological data.

To conclude, the knowledge the community holds must become an integral part of needs assessment and be considered alongside the epidemiological and economic approaches to needs assessments. Together they provide complementary insights into the complexity of needs as experienced by the community and its members. In the light of the issues and problems arising from the various methodologies proposed for health needs assessment, what impact has needs assessment had upon the policies and practices of the National Health Service?

The impact of health needs assessment

The government saw health needs assessment as a tool to help purchasers understand the needs of their populations and inform resource allocation decisions. The process of resource allocation itself has been made more visible with the advent of the internal market which, in turn, has increased both the demand for more accurate information and the need for accountable decision making. Ideally DHAs should develop the public's understanding of the purchasing dilemmas and constraints the health service face, so following consultation, resources could be used in an effective manner which meets the public's needs. Health needs assessment could support this process through the provision of methods for both consultation and data collection, but first a number of conceptual and practical problems currently facing the NHS must be addressed.

First, the objectives of the health service ought to be set within a shared value framework, which provides a common understanding of need and the values upon which resource allocation should be based. Although government guidance on health needs assessment has been available since 1991, its impact upon the health services has been limited. Some commentators question whether or not the guidance provided has really laid the foundations for a true assessment of need. Bradshaw writes

> It does not appear from the early discussion of health needs assessment or from documents supporting the process that it will lead to a change in the attention given by the health service to distributional and equity considerations. Needs assessment has emerged from and quickly settled into the language of priority setting, economic efficiency [and] cost effectiveness.
>
> (Bradshaw 1994: 55)

There are a number of possible reasons for this resistance to the role of health needs assessment. First, providers tend to shy away from the costs of reallocating resources, as they have 'considerable resources committed in plant and staff and these cannot be altered suddenly' (Pickin and St Leger 1993: 182). This together with the vested interests of some providers in maintaining the status quo and the service-led approach, could make the implementation of any change suggested by the findings of a health needs assessment difficult to achieve.

Purchasers also face practical issues such as lack of guidance, lack of resources (human and financial), and the time to undertake comprehensive health needs assessment. At present there is still uncertainty about how to go about undertaking a health needs assessment, the guidance given so far being ambiguous. In addition, advice upon how to relate needs assessment to the planning process is scant and procedures for monitoring DHAs' progress on health needs assessment are not yet in place.

Purchasers lack the financial resources to undertake needs assessment. Conway (1995: 23) cites one survey which discovered that two-thirds of public health directors said they lacked the means to assess need. Although the government promotes cost-effectiveness and public participation, clear guidance on decision making criteria and funding sources is lacking.

There is a shortage of 'pure' research staff within the DHAs to undertake health needs assessment, thus the task is often given to managers with limited research skills, time and resources (Conway 1995: 23). In addition Ong questions the present capacity of public health departments to fulfil their role in needs assessment, and in particular queries their ability to assimilate the issues of unmet need and demand, and the various, sometimes contradictory, understanding of need which the public can present (Ong and Humphris 1994: 79–80).

Finally, Hamilton-Kirkwood and Parry-Langdon suggest the nature and speed of change in the NHS has meant health needs assessment has not been high up the priority list of some providers:

> Centrally determined timetables have caused commissioners to put all of their energies into contract setting with little time for developing 'needologies'. The logical sequence of needs assessment, service specification, and contract setting has been reversed.
>
> (Hamilton-Kirkwood and Parry-Langdon 1993: 8)

There is a possibility, however, that this situation will change. The government is offering support through a needs network for DHAs and the publication of cost-effectiveness bulletins, and has undertaken some needs assessment, for example on diabetes, which could be applied nationally. Also in an attempt to achieve greater purchasing power, DHAs are merging to create purchasing consortia, but they are trying to balance the economic advantages of joint purchasing with a desire to be responsive to local need. Thus some DHAs are developing a locality focus and establishing local offices with responsibility for needs assessment and GP and community liaison. In so doing they are beginning to tap into the knowledge of local people and GPs. This may well develop with the merger of DHAs and Family Health Service Authorities.

Through the GP fundholding scheme general practitioners are already having an impact on needs-led planning, although the effect is potentially counteractive. The success of GP fundholding in terms of the numbers of practices signing up, has resulted in an unanticipated shift towards primary health care (Ham 1994a). However, there is an apparent contradiction between the health needs assessment approach of health authorities and the demand-led approach of GP fundholders. Where DHAs aim to develop a strategic needs-based approach to the health of their population, fundholding GPs, who are only responsible for a range of services to a limited number of patients, are making purchases in direct response to the presenting demands of patients. Thus the scheme undermines the concept of population-based needs planning by allowing GPs to purchase on the basis of individual demand. Since more than a third of the United Kingdom's population are covered by a fundholding practice, and the recently announced extensions to the scheme are intended to take this proportion up to 50 per cent, this means that a sizeable proportion of the population is not covered by an assessment of health needs.

In some parts of the UK these approaches are not so polarized and there are 'a range of approaches to purchasing, which seek to combine the leverage of health authorities with the bite of fundholders' (Ham 1994b: 1032). The Audit Commission has also suggested that what is needed in the future is to ensure that the roles of the health authorities and the GPs are not mutually exclusive and that they work to complement one another: 'The most appropriate compromise could involve authorities encouraging and enabling a bottom-up approach, while checking that the sum total of individual decisions makes sense within broad policy objectives' (Brindle 1993: 17).

To ensure health needs assessment can have an impact on the planning process of the NHS, District Health Authorities need unambiguous guidance on methods and funding to enable them to undertake effective assessments. Methods of collecting epidemiological information must be improved and standardized. The requirement to undertake health needs assessment should be reiterated and strengthened via the implementation of appropriate monitoring and evaluation procedures. To overcome the professional dominance of needs definition, the role of the public must be clarified. Meeting health needs should not be seen as being solely the responsibility of the health services; other organizations and groups should also contribute. Finally, many of the complex issues and quandaries thrown up by health needs assessment could be resolved if the central values upon which health policy is based were clearly defined.

Conclusion

Health needs assessment was intended to inform the strategic and contracting process within the NHS and to contribute to the more effective allocation of health care resources. Responsibility for undertaking health needs assessments was given to the DHAs following the NHS reforms and the creation of the internal market. A possible value framework upon which to base strategic decision making was offered by parallel policy initiatives, including *The Health of the Nation* (Secretary of State for Health 1992), promoting equity issues, a multiagency approach to health care and the benefits of public involvement in defining need. Government guidelines combine epidemiological and economic approaches to health needs assessment. This approach is constrained by its definition of health, dominated by the medical profession, set within the context of existing services and limited by the information available to it. As a result it does little to challenge the perpetuation of service-led provision. Alternative approaches to health needs assessment have challenged the conceptual basis of the epidemiological/medical model, proposing a more holistic definition of health in which subjective perceptions of health and health status are seen to be as valid as those of experts. There are still a number of barriers, however, conceptual and practical, to be overcome before a full picture of health need is achieved. Once these barriers are conquered, health needs assessment has the potential to allow the public increased involvement in planning and the provision of services more committed to meeting their needs. Slowly, the requirement to undertake needs assessment is beginning to affect the policy process, leading purchasers to define their goals and how to achieve them. Should health needs assessment be more widely undertaken, it has the potential to improve the quality of information on need and encourage the sharing of knowledge with other agencies and the public, then perhaps the desired outcome may be achieved.

References

Bradshaw, J. (1994) The conceptualisation and measurement of need – A social policy perspective. In J. Poppay and G. Williams (eds) *Researching People's Health*. London: Routledge.

Brindle, D. (1993) New clash over funds, *The Guardian*, 26 May: 17.

Conway, S. (1995) All out of perspective, *Health Service Journal*, 5 January: 22–3.

Department of Health (1991) *The Patient's Charter – A Summary*. London: HMSO.

Donaldson, C. and Mooney, G. (1991) Needs assessment, priority setting and contracts for health care: An economic view, *British Medical Journal*, 303: 1529–30.

Donaldson, R.J. and Donaldson, L.J. (1993) *Essential Public Health Medicine*. Hingham, MA: Kluwer Academic Publishers.

Ham, C. (1994a) How go the NHS reforms? *British Medical Journal*, 306, 9 January: 77–8.

Ham, C. (1994b) The future of purchasing, *British Medical Journal*, 309, 22 October: 1032–3.

Ham, C. and Spurgeon, P. (1992) *Effective Purchasing*, Health Service Management Centre Discussion Paper 28. Birmingham: HSMC.

Hamilton-Kirkwood, L. and Parry-Langdon, N. (1993) The needs agenda: Health needs assessment, *CCUF Link* (bulletin of the Community Consultation and User Feedback Unit) 2: 8–9.

Institute of Health Services Management and Faculty of Public Health Medicine (1991) *Health for All and the NHS Reforms*. London: IHSM.

Layzell, A. (1994) Perspectives on purchasing: Local and vocal, *Health Service Journal*, 20 January: 28–9.

Lightfoot, J. (1995) Identifying needs and setting priorities: Issues of theory, policy and practice, *Health and Social Care*, 3: 105–14.

Mawhinney, B. (1994) 'Purchasing for health: Involving local people', a speech by Dr Brian Mawhinney MP, Minister for Health, London: HMSO.

NHS Management Executive (1991) *Assessing Health Care Needs*, A DHA project discussion paper. London: NHS Management Executive.

NHS Management Executive (1992) *Local Voices: The Views of Local People in Purchasing for Health*. London: NHS Management Executive.

Ong, B.N. (1993) *The Practice of Health Services Research*. London: Chapman Hall.

Ong, B.N. and Humphris, G. (1994) Prioritizing needs with communities: Rapid appraisal methodologies in health. In J. Poppay and G. Williams (eds) *Researching People's Health*. London: Routledge.

Ong, B.N., Humphris, G., Annett, H. and Rifkin, S. (1991) Rapid appraisal in an urban setting, an example from the developed world, *Social Science Medicine*, 32 (8): 909–15.

Parish, R. (1994) Policy or procrastination? – Part 1: The implications of health of the nation, *Health Education Journal*, 50 (1): 141–5.

Pickin, C. and St Leger, S. (1993) *Assessing Health Need Using the Life Cycle Framework*. Buckingham: Open University Press.

Poppay, J. and Williams, G (eds) (1994) *Researching People's Health*. London: Routledge.

Secretary of State for Health (1991) *The Health of the Nation: A Strategy for Health in England*. London: HMSO.

Southern Community Health Research Unit (1991) *Planning Health Communities: A Guide to Doing Needs Assessment*. Bedford Park, Australia: Flinders Press.

Wainwright, D. (1994) On the waterfront, *Health Service Journal*, 7 July: 28–9.

Whitting, D.S. (1994) How do you take the consumer's view into account? *The Health Summary*, July/August: 9–10.

Wilkin, D., Hallam, L. and Doggett, M.A. (1992) *Measures of Need and Outcome for Primary Health Care*. Oxford: Oxford University Press.

6

JANIE PERCY-SMITH

ASSESSING COMMUNITY NEEDS

Introduction

Community needs assessments take as their starting point neither services nor individuals, but rather communities as collectivities which have needs that both include, and go beyond, the aggregated needs of individuals. The motivations for undertaking community needs assessments are as varied as communities and reflect the diversity of agencies interested in community needs assessment. This diversity is reflected in the range of methods available.

This chapter will begin with an overview of the context within which community needs assessments are taking place, focusing on changes in public sector management and the delivery of local services, recent urban policy initiatives, the revival of interest in aspects of community development and the restoration of the concept of community to the canon of political values. I will then go on to consider what constitutes a community needs assessment before examining some theoretical and conceptual issues associated with the notion of community. Next I will examine the range of methods and methodologies used in assessing community needs and the situations in which different methods are more or less appropriate and useful. Finally, I will identify the range of possible applications of community needs assessments and consider in detail the implications for community needs assessments of a community development approach.

Context

Assessments of community needs are not new. They have, since the 1960s, been used by community practitioners as a means of 'getting to know their patch' and by community workers and community organizations as an important initial step down the community development road. More recently, however, community needs assessments, and similar exercises such as social audits and community profiles (see Hawtin *et al.* 1994), have increasingly been used not only by community-based workers and community organizations, but also by statutory bodies such as local authorities, health authorities, training and enterprise councils and urban regeneration partnership agencies. Community needs assessments are no longer seen solely as a community development tool, but also as an important element in the planning and delivery of services to localities.

There are four main reasons why community needs assessments are moving from being a peripheral activity to a mainstream activity. They relate to changes in the way public services are managed and delivered; recent developments in urban policy; a revival of the notion of community development; and a rediscovery at the political and ideological level of the concept of community. These will be discussed in turn.

Changes in the management and delivery of public services

Since the late 1970s Britain has witnessed considerable change in the way in which public services are managed and delivered (see, for example, Hood 1991; Stoker 1991; Clarke and Stewart 1992; Stewart and Walsh 1992). Some of these changes have been driven from central government, others from local government. Underpinning all the changes has been a desire to shift public services away from what was, arguably, a producer-led system to one in which the needs and wishes of users of public services are responded to more effectively. The Conservative administrations since 1979 have sought to achieve this through the imposition on public services of some of what they see as the disciplines of the market. Thus we have seen the introduction of compulsory competitive tendering (CCT) for a range of local authority services; the separation of purchaser and provider functions within health authorities; and the development of an 'enabling' role for local authorities rather than that of direct provider of services. At the same time public bodies have been increasingly required to demonstrate their effectiveness to service users through the publication of Citizen's and Patient's Charter performance indicators (HMSO 1991).

At the level of the local authority or health authority, there has been a desire on the part of at least some to respond to criticisms that public services are overly bureaucratic, remote and unresponsive to users' needs. At the same time resource constraints have forced many agencies to re-examine the allocation of resources and review the effectiveness of the services that they provide. Also a rising tide of poverty and disadvantage in some areas has meant that local authorities in particular have tried to address increasing inequalities through the use of anti-poverty strategies which seek to redirect resources to those most in need in recognition of the fact that the consumerist approach to the delivery of public services leaves the most disadvantaged even worse off.

As a result a number of local authorities have attempted to decentralize the delivery of services to neighbourhood offices and some have accompanied this with an element of devolution of power (Burns *et al.* 1994). The aim of decentralized service provision is to ensure that services are more responsive to the specific needs of people in the neighbourhoods which they serve. To assist in this process a number of authorities have undertaken local needs assessments to underpin new decentralized service provision. The desire to target scarce resources on those in most need has also necessitated assessments of need although these have tended to be at city, borough and district level rather than community level.

Developments in urban policy

In addition to these broad changes in the management and delivery of public services, recent urban policy initiatives have stressed the importance of community participation and empowerment (Colenutt and Cutten 1993). During the 1980s urban policy was very much dominated by a concern to address the physical dereliction of many run-down inner city areas. Hence the plethora of property-based initiatives such as Enterprise Zones and Urban Development Corporations. By the end of the 1980s there appeared to be an increasing awareness that sustainable urban regeneration required not only the rebuilding of the physical infrastructure but also the rebuilding of the communities that had been affected by urban disadvantage. In addition there has been growing concern that urban regeneration initiatives have been poorly coordinated and have lacked an input from the communities affected. As a result the late 1980s and early 1990s saw a number of initiatives which were intended to ensure better coordination (notably City Action Teams) and to give the community a more active role in the development of initiatives (notably City Challenge). Most recently the Single Regeneration Budget (SRB) has attempted to achieve both of these objectives by incorporating most regeneration monies into a single budget which can be accessed by local partnerships through competitive bids. Local SRB partnerships typically include representation from the community and voluntary sector and there is a clear requirement for SRB bids to demonstrate an understanding of local needs and to show how they plan to involve and consult with communities (Department of the Environment 1995). This has resulted in an upsurge of community needs assessments both as part of the process of preparation of SRB bids and also to provide baseline information of use in monitoring and evaluating the effectiveness of programmes.

However, many of the community needs assessments undertaken in relation to these initiatives have been criticized for being cursory, cosmetic exercises carried out in impossibly short timescales with only minimal participation by and consultation with the community (Colenutt and Cutten 1993). Nevertheless, they have contributed to an environment within which community needs assessments are becoming accepted as legitimate, even essential, elements in the policy process.

Community development

Related, in part, to both the changes in the management and delivery of public services discussed above and also recent urban policy initiatives has been the revival of interest in community development following a number of years during which it was widely regarded as a fringe, even subversive, activity (AMA 1993). As we have seen, urban policy initiatives such as City Challenge and the SRB require consultation with communities and their participation in partnerships. The setting up of user panels and neighbourhood forums as part of decentralization strategies have also necessitated active participation by members of the community. However these forms of participation and consultation require skills and confidence that are not always present in the most disadvantaged communities. Hence the need for community development work to help communities develop the capacity to participate effectively. The recognition of the importance of community development work has resulted in a further impetus towards the undertaking of community needs assessments as a means of encouraging awareness and building skills and confidence within communities. The implications of the community development approach for the way in which community needs assessments are carried out are considered below.

The rediscovery of community

Underpinning all of these developments is the 'rediscovery of community' following the rampant individualism prevalent in the political ideology and policies of the 1980s. In the 1990s we are seeing all shades of the political spectrum embracing the concept of community (Colenutt and Cutten 1993). In particular the 'new' Labour party is adopting many of the ideas developed under the ideological banner of communitarianism. The essential premise of communitarianism is the belief that it is impossible to understand people outside of their social situation. That is, we are all socially constructed and as such are inextricably tied into the communities within which we live and work. Communitarians state that membership of communities entails not only rights (which they argue have dominated political discussion and policy formation) but also responsibilities (Atkinson 1994). This is a clear challenge to the Thatcherite notion of privatized and isolated individuals and their families existing outside of communities and societies each pursuing their own individual well-being. The communitarian argues that the notion of well-being is meaningless outside of the concept of community well-being.

At the same time the post-Thatcherite Conservative party has sought to soften the harsh individualism of the 1980s by giving increasing emphasis to active citizens and building community capacity (Milne 1994). It is tempting to regard this renewed interest in community with a degree of cynicism given the contribution of government policies to the creation of disadvantaged and socially excluded communities and attempts to marginalize and bypass local democratic institutions. Nevertheless these developments have provided a context within which community needs assessments are increasingly recognized as having a role not only in relation to community development but also as a source of useful information for the development and evaluation of policy more generally.

What is a community needs assessment?

There is no single model of what constitutes a community needs assessment and therefore no snappy definition can be proffered. To say that it is a description of the needs of a community is to say very little. For that reason it may be more useful to try to answer some key questions, namely: what kinds of community? who does community needs assessments and why? what kinds of methods are used? what types of needs are assessed?

Communities whose needs are assessed may be either geographically located (e.g. a housing estate or a village) or a community of interest that may or may not inhabit the same physical space (e.g. people with disabilities or an ethnic minority group). Community needs assessments may take place in communities of varying sizes (e.g. a few streets, a neighbourhood, a ward) and varying levels of community organization, development and degrees of social cohesion. The difficulties associated with the use of the term community are discussed below.

Community needs assessments are undertaken by a variety of organizations including: communities themselves, often with the help of a community worker; community practitioners such as health visitors or social workers; statutory agencies such as local authorities (either a single department or corporately) and health authorities; faith groups; voluntary agencies; or a partnership of two or more of these.

The motivations for undertaking community needs assessments are as varied as the organizations that initiate them. They include: providing supporting evidence for a community campaign or to underpin a bid for resources; providing a 'way in' to a community for a newly appointed community practitioner; generating information of relevance to the planning and delivery of local services or to feed into corporate strategic planning processes; setting a baseline against which improvements and service effectiveness can be measured; and as a means of building community capacity, confidence and awareness as part of a process of community development.

Community needs assessments typically make use of one or more different methods. These may be quantitative or qualitative, participative or non-participative, and may utilize either primary or secondary data. The range of methods that might be used in community needs assessment is discussed in detail below.

The scope of community needs assessments may be more or less comprehensive in terms of the range of needs analysed. So, for example, the primary focus might be health and welfare needs or it may try to cover all or most aspects of life within the community. Those community needs assessments which are carried out in a community development context are more likely to be comprehensive, recognizing the interconnected nature of need and disadvantage. In addition needs assessments of this type tend to go beyond needs to include an analysis of the strengths and capacities of the community.

However, what is perhaps distinctive about community needs assessments is that they tend *not* to start with a particular set of services or a policy area and then find out how many and what kind of people need those services. Rather, in keeping with the move towards needs-led rather than producer-led services, they begin with people. This is important since the service-led approach is inevitably conservative and will, at best, result in marginal improvements to existing services. It is unlikely to generate information about needs for an entirely different range of services. To start with people is a more difficult but more radical approach. It may result in new categories of needs being identified and may challenge departmental/agency boundaries and the way in which services are currently provided. Such an approach is frequently criticized for raising expectations which cannot then be met by statutory bodies who are short of resources. This may be the case but it is important, nevertheless, to remember that it is not the community needs assessment that creates the need but merely allows an existing need to be articulated and to become visible. Furthermore, as I have argued elsewhere (Percy-Smith 1992), need does not entail a right to having that need met. Difficult decisions about which needs are to be met and at what level will still have to be made.

In reality, in the most disadvantaged communities the opposite problem – chronically low expectations and a resigned acceptance of high levels of social and personal disadvantage – may be more prevalent. A community needs assessment that is undertaken without an overarching theory of what constitutes need may run the risk of simply perpetuating a situation in which the needs of the most disadvantaged are insufficiently recognized. However researchers who, in undertaking a community needs assessment, provide people with cues or prompts that enable them to recognize their needs as such and legitimize their articulation, can be accused of unduly influencing the outcome of the research process and giving too much weight to the views of experts and professionals (Graham and Jones 1992).

The second distinctive feature of community needs assessments is that the focus is the collective needs of the community rather than just the needs of individuals added together. This is important since it allows for the possibility of negotiating between different groups within the community what is in the best interest of the community as a whole. It also allows for a recognition of the way in which concentrations of disadvantaged people living in the same area can result in new kinds of disadvantage that can only be addressed at the level of the community. For example low income levels, and therefore spending power, in a community can result in local shops closing down, creating problems of access; low levels of educational achievement in a local school can lead to better off parents sending their children to different schools outside the local community, exacerbating tensions and resulting in fewer pupils, and therefore resources, going to the local school.

Theoretical and conceptual issues

There are two important conceptual issues which need to be discussed in the context of community needs assessments. The first is what we mean by community and the second, related, issue is the relationship of individuals to communities and the extent to which it is possible to talk about communities having needs.

The concept of community is contested (Plant *et al.* 1980: 208; Taylor 1992: 3–4; Butcher *et al.* 1993: 11–18). There are numerous ways in which community can be defined and conceptualized. However the essential thread that runs through most definitions is the idea of a group of people who are linked in some way. For the purposes of this discussion there are two main kinds of common links: those that arise from people living in the same area or neighbourhood and those that arise from people having one or more shared characteristics. The first type of community we can refer to as a spatial community and the second as a community of interest.

Spatial communities are made up of all those people who live and, possibly, work in the same geographical location, for example a housing estate or village. However, we might also want to define communities in terms of an administrative area such as an electoral ward, social services area or school catchment area.

A community of interest consists of people who, whether or not they live in the same geographical location, share certain characteristics, for example children or people with disabilities. It is possible that as a result of increased geographical mobility and fragmentation of traditional communities that communities of interest (facilitated perhaps by electronic means of communication) will emerge as more significant than spatial communities in the future. However for most people the area in which they live and work and where their children go to school still provides the closest approximation to community. But it is important to recognize that this may be a culturally specific experience in the sense that for some groups, for example Moslem people living in Britain, their community is geographically dispersed but nevertheless constitutes a more or less cohesive grouping which shares at least some common needs and interests.

However there are problems with both of these approaches. In both cases it is assumed that by virtue of the fact that people have something in common (living in the same area or sharing a particular characteristic) that they do in fact constitute a community with shared or common interests. In reality the truth may be that this is the only aspect of their lives that they hold in common and they are divided by more than unites them. In other words we are assigning a commonality of interest to a group of essentially unconnected individuals.

Part of the problem arises out of the fact that the concept of community has both a descriptive and a normative element. Community is a positive buzzword; it is seen to be a 'good thing'. Indeed, part of the rationale for undertaking community needs assessments is supportive of that normative aspect of community. However communities are not and never have been (despite nostalgic evocations of a lost golden age of community) homogenous and without divisions and conflicts. This does not necessarily invalidate the concept of community nor the relevance of community needs assessments but should rather alert us to the possibility or even likelihood of 'communities within communities' and the dangers of imputing needs to people on the basis of flimsy evidence drawn from an unrepresentative sample of the population to be researched.

It should also alert us to the need to be sensitive in the drawing of bound-aries around communities so that they do, as far as possible, reflect people's own perceptions of the extent of their community. There is evidence to suggest that on the whole people identify with quite local areas although this may be different for different purposes and may not be particularly well-defined (Blackman 1995: 143). The common understanding in a locality or within a population group of what constitutes the community will have an effect on the size of the community that is chosen for the purposes of a needs assess-ment and the methods to be used (see below). It may also be necessary in undertaking a needs assessment in a community which is very divided to employ a range of different research methods that are appropriate to the differ-ent groups comprising the community. The most obvious example is a multi-cultural community where, at the very least, steps may have to be taken to translate survey materials and to ensure that they are culturally relevant and appropriate. However it may also be necessary to use different research methods in order to gain access to certain groups. For example a needs assess-ment based around a series of mixed focus groups may effectively exclude some Asian women from participating. If this is the case then their views will need to be obtained using a different method.

Communities of all types are made up of individuals who, in turn, are typi-cally members of more than one community. What then is the relationship of individuals to communities? Are communities different from a simple aggre-gation of the individuals who constitute them? Can communities really be said to have needs?

These are difficult issues. What is important for the purpose of the present discussion is to recognize that community needs assessments are usually intended to go beyond a simple aggregation of needs as identified by indi-viduals. There are two reasons for this. First, there is evidence to suggest that the responses that individuals give to, for example, social surveys are different from those which are articulated through group discussions. Not surprisingly in a one-to-one situation involving an interviewee and an interviewer the interviewee will give an immediate and often unconsidered response whereas in a group discussion there is the opportunity for respondents to reflect and change their minds as a result of listening to the views of others. This is an important process for anyone concerned with the building of cohesive com-munities since it can contribute to greater understanding and toleration of diversity and difference.

Second, a list of needs as a result of interviewing or surveying individuals is likely to be a long list with no indication of what the priorities are or ought to be. Group discussion can lead to individuals within communities agreeing a set of priorities for the community as a whole which may not accord with their own individual set of priorities. Again this is an important contribution to the building of community consciousness.

These two examples suggest that a community is more than or different to the sum of the individuals who make it up and to that extent can be said to have needs that are, in some respects, different from those of the individuals who comprise them.

Methods and methodologies

As has been suggested above there are a wide range of different methods for and approaches to assessing community needs. These have been referred to in the chapter on methodologies for needs assessment and include: analysis of secondary data and social indicators; social surveys; focus groups; and mapping techniques (see also Lloyd *et al.* 1991; Burton 1993; Hawtin *et al.* 1994). In broad terms these different methods can be located along the three dimensions identified in Figure 6.1.

Which method or combination of methods is selected will depend on three key factors: the type of community whose needs are to be assessed; the purpose, aims and objectives of the needs assessment; and the resources available. It is worth considering briefly how some different answers to the above questions might affect the choice of methods.

The nature of the community

A small, spatially located community with an existing infrastructure of community organizations lends itself most readily to the collection of new (primary) data, possibly using qualitative methods, with a high degree of participation by members of the community. By contrast a community of interest that is geographically dispersed, e.g. people with disabilities spread throughout a city, might require a more quantitative, less participative approach. The level of development of the community to be researched is an important consideration. It is very difficult (and probably ineffective) to try to undertake participative research in communities with little or no community infrastructure in the form of community organizations or history of community organizing. It may, in this situation, be more appropriate to use the findings from the needs assessment as a catalyst for more wide-ranging community development work.

Purpose, aims and objectives

A community needs assessment, as we have seen, may be initiated by a range of different agencies for a variety of different purposes. A clear set of aims and objectives for the needs assessment is crucial before decisions can be made about the most appropriate methods to be used. For example, a community organization may wish to undertake a needs assessment in order to demonstrate to statutory agencies and service providers that they require more

Figure 6.1 Methods of assessment

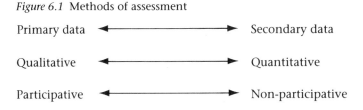

or different services. Or a local partnership may wish to provide a rationale for including a particular community in a bid for urban regeneration resources. In both these cases the need to persuade others might require the use of quantitative data, drawn from either primary or secondary sources, or a combination of the two. It is still the case that quantitative data – 'hard' statistics – is seen to be more reliable and to have greater authority than 'softer' qualitative information. If this is the main purpose of the exercise then quantitative methods may be best.

By contrast if the main purpose of the needs assessment is to begin a process of community development then a highly participative, qualitative approach involving in-depth interviews, focus groups and public meetings might be called for. The extent to which the community can determine the research focus will depend on the extent of community development work that has already taken place.

Resources available

Community needs assessments can be highly resource intensive. The group or agency initiating the research must include in their planning an assessment of the resources available to them in terms of:

- money;
- time – has the needs assessment got to be finished by a particular date?
- expertise, e.g. research design, project management, computing, data analysis, interviewing, report-writing;
- people – to undertake field work, input data, etc.;
- equipment, e.g. computers, photocopier, etc.

A local authority wanting to undertake a community needs assessment as part of a bid for funds may have resources in terms of money, expertise and equipment, but lack time and people to undertake fieldwork. In this situation it may decide to make use of existing secondary data to support its case but to manipulate that data using its computing experts to 'add value' to the data. This might involve mapping data to compare the target area with other areas (see, for example, Cripps and Pate 1991) or to undertake cluster analysis in order to demonstrate the interrelated nature of the disadvantages suffered by particular members of the community (see, for example, Smith 1995).

By contrast a community group is likely to lack resources in terms of money, expertise and equipment, but have abundant supplies of time and people. In this situation a social survey involving face to face in-depth interviews or a series of focus group discussions may be more appropriate.

Applications

As we have seen community needs assessments are carried out by statutory and voluntary and community agencies for a range of different purposes. Statutory agencies can use information derived from community needs assessments to feed into the strategic planning process through the identification of areas or groups requiring priority action or to determine areas requiring targeting of resources. In many cases this will be part of an anti-poverty strategy. In addition information from community needs assessments can be used as the basis for improving service delivery at a neighbourhood level perhaps as part of a decentralization strategy. Related to this is the use of community needs assessments as the basis for drawing up area-based action plans. Community needs assessments can also be used to provide baseline information against which progress can be measured and the effectiveness of interventions assessed. Such baseline information may also be important for forecasting likely levels of need in the future. And, finally as we have seen, community needs assessments are increasingly being used to provide the rationale for bids for competitive funding and as the basis for the development of appropriate and effective regeneration programmes.

Voluntary and community organizations have typically used community needs assessments as a way of demonstrating that there exist in the community needs that are not currently being met and/or shortfalls in service or as part of campaigns for or against new initiatives. Statutory, voluntary and community organizations have all used community needs assessments as a part of the community development process. It is this application of community needs assessments on which I will now focus.

Community needs assessment in a community development context

Given that much community needs assessment research is with communities that are characterized by multiple disadvantage it is important that we can justify not only the outcome of the research, but also the fact of the research in terms of the benefit to the community to be studied. One obvious benefit to the community is where needs are identified and appropriate resources or services are then forthcoming as a result. However this may not always be the case, especially where the research is undertaken in order to underpin what might be a speculative funding bid. Of course such research must still take place if chances of success are judged to be high enough to justify the expenditure of resources and the 'costs' to the community that may be involved. However where there can be no cast iron guarantee of direct benefit then it is especially important that research is undertaken in such a way that the community still obtains some benefit from it. Undertaking the research using a community development approach can offer such a benefit to the community.

What are the key elements of a community development approach? First it is holistic. By that I mean that it works on all fronts simultaneously, recognizing that people living in disadvantaged communities are affected by a multiplicity of different problems which are mutually reinforcing and not easily disentangled.

Second it is multiagency, operating at two levels. Following on from the last point, since we are addressing a multiplicity of different problems, a multiplicity of agencies with responsibility for those problem areas should be involved. Also, the problems identified are likely to be too great and require too many resources to be handled by a single statutory agency or by the market or by the voluntary sector. Resources will need to be found from all these and other sources.

The third element of a community development approach is that it should involve, enable and, ultimately, empower local people. This is possibly the hardest part of the process but the most important in terms of the long term sustainability of any improvements that are put in place.

The fourth element is that the research should be ethical. This entails obtaining the informed consent of those who are to be involved as research subjects in the community needs assessment. This suggests the need for appropriate preliminary work with the community in order to articulate the aims, objectives and purposes for doing the research so that consent, if it is granted, can properly be said to have been informed consent. The research should also be purposeful. In other words there should be a good reason for undertaking the community needs assessment and this should be made known to people. Finally, the anticipated benefits of the research should be proportional to the costs or risks. In other words the community might reasonably expect to benefit in some way from the community needs assessment and the benefit should outweigh the cost to them.

If we accept the need for a community development approach, then those key elements that we have identified give us the beginnings of an agenda in terms of issues to be researched, styles of research that are appropriate and the uses to which community needs assessments are put.

Issues to be researched

Given the multiple nature of disadvantage, the fact that communities do not perceive the problems that they confront in their everyday lives along agency or departmental lines and the need to be holistic as the community development approach suggests, there is a strong case for community needs assessments to be comprehensive and inclusive in scope.

If research is to meet the objective of being empowering or, at the very least, not disempowering, then it is important that in addition to identifying the needs of communities, that questions are also asked which allow the community to demonstrate its strengths, potential and aspirations. Even the most disadvantaged communities can demonstrate strengths such as tenacity and supportive networks and will have aspirations for the future which can and should be brought out through the needs assessment process.

Finally, the most rigorous espousal of the community development approach would suggest that the research agenda for a community needs assessment – the issues to be researched – should emerge from the community rather than being imposed from outside. In practice this can be difficult; the timescale for undertaking community research may be too short to allow the quite lengthy process required to build up a community to the point at which it is able to articulate the issues that it thinks should be the focus for research. Also, as I indicated earlier, the impetus for the research may lie within agencies that have their own agenda which may not be amenable to too much change. Nevertheless it should be possible even within the tightest timescales to carry out some preliminary soundings within the community about what the main issues are which can inform the design of the research.

Styles of research

The requirement to be comprehensive in scope and holistic in approach can be carried through into the research style by selecting a range of different research methods which offer alternative perspectives on the same issue. Thus if we take health as an example, there are a number of different sources of information about the health status of a population all of which are likely to be important in building up a comprehensive picture of the health of a community. First of all there are the secondary data sources which tell us about standardized mortality rates; infant mortality; information on deaths from certain diseases and so on. All of this information – routinely collected by health authorities – is extremely important in building up a picture of one community as compared with others. However what this data will not give us is any indication of those illnesses that people do not die of, are not contagious but which can, nevertheless, blight lives. These diseases include the kinds of chronic illnesses usually treated through GPs and primary care services such as asthma.

It might be possible to obtain information of this kind by talking to GPs and health visitors. Front line service providers are often an important source of detailed information about communities gleaned from their day to day experience of working in those communities. However even this does not tell us very much about the ordinary experiences of people whose lives are limited by ill-health. This information needs to be obtained by talking to the people affected.

If, though, we want to move from descriptions of how things are to how things might be, talking to people as individuals may not be the best approach. To continue with the health example, there is evidence to show that asking people if they are generally satisfied with health services leads to overwhelmingly positive responses, especially among older people. Similarly if we ask people individually how health services might be improved we are likely to get a large number of 'don't know' responses. The issue is simply too large to confront head on. A different approach is required.

Consideration of these points might lead to a set of complementary research methods as follows:

- analysis of secondary data sources in order to compare the community with other communities and to identify problem areas;
- semi-structured interviews with service providers and community representatives to obtain their perceptions of local needs;
- structured interviews with a representative sample of residents to ascertain their views on the needs of the community and local issues;
- focus or discussion groups led by a facilitator to allow informal discussion of ideas, options and possible solutions.

A community needs assessment can attempt to meet the objective of being involving, enabling and empowering by adopting a number of different methods (see also Hawtin *et al.* 1994: Ch. 3). The process can be involving by, for example, recruiting and training local people to undertake interview work; including local residents on a project steering group; interviewing a larger rather than smaller sample; holding a number of focus or discussion groups; consulting widely prior to commencing research and keeping people informed about the progress of the research through regular newsletters or publicity leaflets, including providing information in appropriate ethnic minority languages and recognizing that not everyone is literate.

The process can be enabling if, in participating in the research process, local people acquire new skills (e.g. interviewing, data entry or interpretation of statistical data), fresh insights and new knowledge about their community.

A community needs assessment can be empowering if those involved develop a greater sense of their own worth as a community, are enabled to come together and develop a sense of themselves as a community with at least some common interests, and can see a way to move forward. Facilitating a community's understanding of how they stand in relation to other communities, the development of a shared agenda and a set of clearly defined objectives to work towards can be the first step down the road to sustainable community regeneration and greater self-confidence. Of course what this suggests is that the process of undertaking a community needs assessment might be more important than the research findings themselves. If this is the case, if the primary purpose for undertaking the research is community development, then it is important that enough time is built into the research timetable to allow involvement by local people and the development of skills and the articulation of aspirations.

Conclusions

The increasing use of community needs assessments by both statutory and community organizations has occurred at a time when changes in the management and delivery of public services aimed at making them more responsive, locally based and needs-led have coincided with a concern, at the local level at least, to ensure that services are targeted on those in most need. In addition local authorities and other public agencies are increasingly required to demonstrate their effectiveness especially in relation to meeting needs. At the same time recent urban policy initiatives have stressed the importance of consulting with communities and taking account of their needs in the formulation of regeneration strategies. This has been reinforced by a revival of interest in the concept of community at the ideological and political level and in the practice of community development.

As a result a wide variety of different techniques are currently being used to assess community needs, ranging from essentially quantitative manipulation of secondary data to participative and imaginative qualitative research. I have tried to show in this chapter that all of these techniques can have a place in the conduct of a community needs assessment depending on the type and size of community whose needs are to be assessed, the purpose for undertaking the needs assessment and the resources available.

Community needs assessments can yield information with considerable potential benefit to the agencies that initiate them. For statutory agencies this might include better information on which to make resource allocation decisions, to review and evaluate services or to justify a bid for funding. Many community needs assessments are undertaken as part of a process of community development and I have suggested that as such they should try to conform to certain community development principles, namely that they should be holistic, multiagency, ethical and involving, enabling and empowering of local people.

References

Association of Metropolitan Authorities (AMA) (1993) *Local Authorities and Community Development. A Strategic Opportunity for the 1990s*. London: AMA.

Atkinson, D. (1994) *The Common Sense of Community*. London: Demos.

Blackman, T. (1995) *Urban Policy in Practice*. London: Routledge.

Burns, D., Hambleton, R. and Hoggett, P. (1994) *The Politics of Decentralisation: Revitalising Local Democracy*. Basingstoke: Macmillan.

Burton, P. (1993) *Community Profiling. A Guide to Identifying Local Needs*. Bristol: University of Bristol, School for Advanced Urban Studies.

Butcher, H., Glen, A., Henderson, P. and Smith, J. (eds) (1993) *Community and Public Policy*. Pluto Press, London.

Clarke, M. and Stewart, J (1992) *Citizens and Local Democracy. Empowerment: A Theme for the 1990s*. Luton: Local Government Management Board.

Colenutt, B. and Cutten, A. (1993) Community empowerment in vogue or vain?' *Local Economy*, 9 (3) November: 30–1.

Cripps, E. and Pate, S. (1991) Using GIS to target Cumbria's resources, *Planning Outlook*, 34 (1): 43–9.

Department of the Environment (1995) *Bidding Guidance: A Guide to Bidding for Resources from the Government's Single Regeneration Budget Challenge Fund*. London: DoE.

Graham, H. and Jones, J. (1992) Community development and research, *Community Development Journal*, 27 (3) July: 235–41.

Hawtin, M., Hughes, G. and Percy-Smith, J. (1994) *Community Profiling. Auditing Social Needs*. Open University Press, Buckingham.

HMSO (1991) *The Citizen's Charter: Raising the Standard*, Cm 1599. London: HMSO.

Hood, C. (1991) A public management for all seasons, *Public Administration*, 69 (1): 3–19.

Lloyd, P., Marsden, P. and Scott, D. (eds) (1991) *Researching Voluntary and Community Action. Questions of Policy and Practice*. Wivenhoe: ARVAC.

Milne, K. (1994) Community: the Tories fight back, *New Statesman and Society*, 22 July, 20–1.

Percy-Smith, J. (1992) Auditing social needs, *Policy and Politics*, 20 (1): 29–34.

Plant, R., Lesser, H. and Taylor-Gooby, P. (1980) *Political Philosophy and Social Welfare. Essays on the Normative Basis of Welfare Provision*. London: Routledge and Kegan Paul.

Smith, G. (1995) 'Census data and the Church Urban Fund', unpublished paper, Aston Community Involvement Unit.

Stewart, J. and Walsh, K. (1992) Change in the management of public services, *Public Administration*, 70 (4): 499–518.

Stoker, G. (1991) *The Politics of Local Government*, 2nd edn. London: Macmillan.

Taylor, M. (1992) *Signposts to Community Development*. London: Community Development Foundation.

ASSESSING HOUSING NEEDS

Introduction

Local housing need assessments are based on the assumption that certain people within a defined area have housing problems that can, potentially, be solved. In practice assessments are more of an art than an exact science. Measuring housing need is a complex and difficult undertaking not least because of the problems in defining what we mean by housing, which people can be considered as in need, what the problems are and what are the most appropriate ways of meeting those needs. These are not just technical issues, but involve value judgements which, in turn, reflect political, professional and consumer priorities. Beyond this basic definition of housing need lie further complex dimensions, such as consumer choice and the ability to pay, and households' wishes, desires and aspirations.

Section 8 of the Housing Act 1985 states 'every local authority shall consider housing conditions in their district and the needs of the district with respect to the provision of further housing accommodation'. This chapter explores the development of, and concepts behind, housing needs assessment as envisaged in this Act. Housing need, as with any social need, is essentially concerned with the gap between actual housing and an agreed standard of 'adequate housing'. Therefore, as an understanding of adequate housing is crucial to assessing housing needs, we examine the range of characteristics that relate to this concept including: space; the availability of certain facilities; the condition of the property; the location of the property; access; and the environment.

The context

Local authorities were first required to assess housing needs in their area under the Housing Act 1935. The Act was developed out of concern about households living in overcrowded and poor conditions; it defined overcrowding and required authorities to appraise its extent in their area. A requirement to appraise housing need was also contained in the Housing Act 1957. The Seebohm Report, on *Local Authority and Allied Personal Social Services* (Seebohm 1968), argued that many local authorities had concentrated on issues around council housing to the exclusion of other forms of housing tenure. The report recommended that local authorities should extend their role in housing to include assessment of local housing need. These suggestions were echoed the following year in the Cullingworth Report on council housing (Central Housing Advisory Committee 1969).

The concept of a local housing strategy made its appearance in 1977 when the Labour government published a fundamental review of housing finance (DoE 1977) which addressed the development of local, broadly based housing strategies. These strategies were to have two elements: a Housing Investment Programme (HIP) that specified the local authorities' spending proposals, and a housing strategy statement which provided a justification for the HIP. Authorities were expected to assess local housing needs objectively and comprehensively. Similar systems were set up in Scotland (Housing Plans) and Wales (Housing Strategies and Operational Plans).

In the short term the HIP system resulted in a more systematic approach to information gathering and also in developing and reviewing housing policies (Morris 1980). However, it soon became evident that there was minimal political commitment to what came to be seen as little more than a technocratic exercise. Other problems emerged throughout the 1980s such as the difficulty of developing a comprehensive strategy and a realization that a thorough needs assessment was beyond the means of most local authorities. It was also felt that because of a lack of local information the necessity to assess needs slowed down the housing development process (Hoyle and Brindley 1983).

Since 1979 housing investment has been progressively reduced, and local authorities' capital programmes have switched from new build (based on some estimate of need) to little more than renovation and refurbishment of existing properties. In addition the total stock available to councils for rehousing people has dropped in Great Britain from 6.2 million in 1983 to 4.9 million in 1993. As a result few local authorities felt it worthwhile to undertake detailed local housing needs assessments whilst the means to meet those needs were becoming more and more scarce and their discretion over housing allocations reduced. Many local authorities also dismissed the relevance of housing needs assessments to longer term planning in part since funding for many capital schemes was only being awarded on an annual basis. Focus of attention, therefore, shifted from a strategic view of housing investment to detailed concerns about projects and short term financial implications.

Despite the criticisms of the HIP system during the mid-1980s, some support for the adoption of local housing plans based on local needs assessment began to emerge. For example, in 1985 the Labour Party National Executive Committee proposed: 'to give councils the key role in housing'. They went on:

They will be responsible for planning housing development: not just council housing but for the private sector, including housing associations and private building for owner-occupation . . . Under our proposals, local authorities will be required to draw up *local housing plans* to assess housing demand, estimate public and private building performance, and provide five-year rolling plans tailored to local needs.

(Labour Party NEC 1985)

The Association of Metropolitan Authorities (AMA) published a booklet in 1987 recommending the adoption of a new and standardized approach to the planning and implementation of local housing policies. It recognized that the foundation of a good housing strategy should be an analysis of a wide range of qualitative and quantitative data, along with the involvement of the community in expressing demands and making choices (AMA 1987). The AMA, and others who supported local housing plans (Merrett 1986; AMA 1987), felt that such plans should be need, rather than resource-led, based on a four or five-year rolling programme and the participation and views of other organizations, including the community itself, should be ensured in drawing up plans.

A few local authorities drew up a 'desirable strategy' based on a thorough assessment of local housing need in addition to their HIP bid which worked within shorter term financial constraints (Cole and Goodchild 1995). These alternative strategies often had a political, rather than technical base, demonstrating the possible role for the local authority within a more sympathetic political and financial framework.

New strategic role

Since 1985 government policy has sought to give local housing authorities a more strategic and coordinating role, encouraging them to act as enablers in relation to housing, assisting other agencies to provide low cost housing. The direct provision and management function of local authorities has been eroded by the 'Right to Buy' legislation, the reduction in capital borrowing allowances to levels where authorities are unable to build more homes and the introduction of compulsory competitive tendering of housing management. The Department of the Environment's White Paper in 1987, *Housing: The Government's Proposals*, suggested that housing associations take over the provision of new social housing and local authorities adopt a strategic role which would include:

- identifying housing needs and demands;
- identifying resources and powers available to meet the need;
- preparing and monitoring a local housing strategy, based on the demand and using available resources and powers;
- working with other agencies to implement the strategy.

The Audit Commission in 1992 added its voice to the view that local housing strategies should be firmly based on an assessment of housing needs, especially given the changing role of local authorities (Audit Commission 1992). It stressed that the new role requires local authorities to be more fully informed about meeting the housing needs by all relevant agencies and sectors, rather than confining themselves to only those to which they could respond as land-lords.

The government, since 1985, has also repeatedly expressed its view on the importance of housing needs assessments. The Housing Act 1985 (and the Housing (Scotland) Act 1987) gave local authorities the statutory duty to review the housing needs of residents in their area. The Local Government and Housing Act 1989 introduced a new system of housing finance which included among its objectives that of bringing about a distribution of capital expenditure reflective of national and local need and to provide a sound basis for local authorities to plan their capital programmes with confidence (Malpass and Murie 1994). Also the 1992 HIP guidance to local authorities from the Department of the Environment states that authorities are required to explore needs and resources on an informed basis, drawing on appropriate sources of information and even undertaking primary research.

The new financial system is, however, seen by many as little better than the former HIP approach in encouraging needs assessment. Margaret Singh, Chair of the Association of District Councils, has written:

> By now the whole process has become a series of rituals . . . The more we investigate housing need, produce strategies for dealing with it and draw up ever more sophisticated ways of measuring performance the fewer resources we are given to dealing with needs . . . Does the process *really* serve to inform ministers about the housing needs of different areas? . . . The most urgent need might be for new rented housing, but it would be a foolish council that made that the centre of its strategy, let alone propose to build such housing itself.
>
> (Singh 1994)

For the past 60 years local authorities have had a statutory requirement to appraise local housing need which underpins their fundamental role to ensure that the basic needs of their citizens are met. Prior to the 1980s the assumption was that unmet need would be met by the authority in its capacity as providers and managers of low cost housing. Now, however, that assumption is overturned with the government's proposals that 'the future role of local authorities will be a strategic one – identifying housing needs and demands, and encouraging innovative methods of provision by other bodies to meet those needs' (DoE 1987).

The consequences of local authorities' inability to provide low cost housing, and whether the market is capable of supporting other means of provision, is beyond the scope of this chapter. However the uncertainty of authorities about their ability to meet demand (let alone need) effectively is one factor which has led to local housing needs assessments having a somewhat chequered history. A more fundamental factor though, in mitigating against rigorous and robust housing needs assessments, is the intrinsic problem of identifying and deciding what is meant by the term 'housing need'.

The concept of housing need

The concept of housing need has been defined as 'those households falling below defined minimum standards of accommodation' (DoE 1980). Housing need therefore refers to the notional gap between the needs of households in a designated area and the supply of appropriate housing. However on another level defining housing needs becomes more problematic. How do we interpret the words household and housing? What are minimum standards? Who defines these terms?

The eligible household

Unlike the assessment of other needs, such as health or social care, housing is concerned less with individual need than 'the household' as a basic unit of measurement. Decisions therefore must be made about what constitutes a 'household'. Household size is, to some extent, determined by current norms and expectations with a shift away from 'traditional' married couples towards a greater proportion of single people, lone parents and elderly person households.

There are legally defined households for which the state accepts responsibility to provide accommodation, currently laid down through the Housing (Homeless Persons) Act 1977. They are principally married couples and parents with children, together with some single people with special requirements. The Children Act 1990 and the NHS and Community Care Act 1990 have also specified types of households for whom local authorities have housing responsibility. Some, however, have argued for the list to be significantly wider, including all single people, or indeed everyone who wishes to live independently and safely.

Demonstrating a *need* for housing may not in itself be sufficient to secure *access* to suitable housing. In most cases households in housing need will also have to demonstrate that they meet eligibility criteria which restricts access to housing resources to those whose needs are recognized by providers. Mortgages, for example, are, in practice, only accessible to households earning over a certain level.

Local authorities have a statutory duty to give preference when allocating accommodation to those who are overcrowded, those with large families, people living in unsatisfactory conditions and those found to be homeless through slum clearance and fire and flood. However, applicants to local authority housing usually have to satisfy some eligibility requirements such as residence in the authority area for a minimum period, age, marital status, being an owner occupier and being in debt in respect of current or previous residence.

'Adequate housing'

It is widely agreed that adequate housing is vital to human health and well-being (Arblaster and Hawtin 1993). However housing can be understood as simply any form of shelter through to a complex arrangement of homes in a neighbourhood. Similarly, a detailed understanding of what may be considered 'adequate' is necessary for any assessment to be made. Both terms are relatively determined both culturally and over time.

Doyal and Gough (1991) state that there are three characteristics related to housing which, if not met, are inimitable to the health of its inhabitants. First, the property must afford protection from the extremes of the climate, from exposure, and from pests and disease-carrying vectors. Second, the accommodation must provide sanitation in the provision of clean water and disposal of sewage. Third, the dwelling must not be overcrowded leading to excessive social demands and lack of privacy.

It is unlikely that the importance of these three characteristics would be disputed in our society today. However, defining housing only in terms of basic shelter is only one very narrow definition. The *Faith in the City* report defined housing in a broad sense; it stated,

> A house is more than bricks and mortar, it is more than a roof over one's head. Decent housing is a place that is dry and warm and in reasonable repair. It also means security, privacy, sufficient space; a place where people can grow, make choices, become more whole people. It relates to the environment in which the house is located.
>
> (Archbishop of Canterbury Commission 1985)

A wide definition of housing, therefore, could include the following characteristics:

- space requirements – in terms of size of rooms. Gardens or private outdoor space are also considered as necessary by some (Mellinger 1994);
- certain facilities and amenities – such as those necessary to meet hygiene standards or to cope with old age or infirmity;
- condition of property – to provide protection from extremes of the climate, to be damp and draught free, to be safe to live in, and offer reasonable privacy in terms of preventing noise, cooking smells and being overlooked;
- supervision – the support attached to certain housing types provided by some housing authorities and associations can be essential if some people are to remain in the community;
- suitable location – proximity to work, relatives or carers; lack of postcode discrimination; and a safe environment are important for economic and social reasons. Some argue that, as far as practicable, elderly and disabled and families with young children are usually better accommodated nearer to ground floor levels;
- access – to suitable accommodation may be denied because of ineligibility due to personal circumstances, physical suitability or the costs associated with the accommodation. Separate pedestrian and vehicle access may be necessary with parking accommodation close to the property;
- management/control – security of tenure, and the right to control the management of the property are important aspects of adequate housing;
- environmental issues – are a growing concern involving not only energy and

water saving measures but also the reduction of CO_2 emissions, use of sustainable and healthy materials, waste recycling and suitable planning to reduce motor transport.

To define households as being 'adequately' housed implies that the conditions in which they live meet a certain defined level of standard, below which they are considered in need. If the broader definition of housing is taken, those standards must be applied to all of the above list of housing characteristics. To define 'adequate housing' therefore, requires not only an agreement about the range of characteristics to be used, but also the level of standard which is acceptable.

Standards are constantly changing, however minimum acceptable housing standards are laid down by legislation and government guidance. Minimum statutory standards applying to all housing characteristics are complex, however they include: an 'unfitness standard' for existing dwellings; building regulations for new housing; design guidance for special needs housing; housing benefit regulations; tenancy conditions as set out in various acts of parliament and case judgements; and access to assistance to accommodation by the local authority contained in the homelessness legislation.

Higher levels of standard will inevitably mean that more households will be assessed as being in need. If those needs are to be met by the state, the higher levels of standard will depend both on what society deems is acceptable and is prepared to pay for. However if those needs are not to be met by the state, but by market forces, it may be argued that there is no necessity to set higher standards, and even the need to set minimum standards is in question.

Objective or subjective definitions

Defining housing need is, as we have seen, initially dependent on a clear identification of the terms 'household' and 'housing'. However within that identification there needs to be an agreement about which households are eligible to form an independent household, and what characteristics and standards are considered to constitute 'adequate' housing. A further issue therefore relates to whether this interpretation of housing needs can, or should be, defined and assessed by housing professionals or whether consumers' subjective preferences should also be taken into account.

Bradshaw (1972) identifies four approaches to needs:

- normative needs,
- felt needs,
- expressed needs,
- comparative needs.

Normative need draws on expert knowledge to define minimum, or adequate, standards which are then used as the basis for defining need. For example, building and fitness standards are set by a technical and political process, and inspections carried out by those applying the current normative values of society. Standards using only a normative approach can, however, become élitist with a danger of being set at a level that is incompatible with the demand. The cost of renovating a dwelling regarded as substandard may be prohibitive for some households.

Felt needs are the aspirations and expectations of people themselves. Central heating is, for example, considered a necessity by many. This relies on insight into people's own situations. However lack of knowledge and technical expertise may result in individuals not recognizing that they do in fact have a need.

The approach to expressed needs is based on the behaviour of individuals. This may include the use of housing waiting lists, uptake of the 'Right to Buy' and 'Right to Manage', and changes in house prices. Many policy decisions are in fact based largely on expressed needs. However expressed needs reflect current provision and availability and may not constitute an accurate picture of need as such. For example council house waiting lists (expressed need) have often in the past provided the basis on which housing needs assessments have been made. However, it is now widely recognized that they rarely reflect true need in that many people will only apply if they believe they are likely to be rehoused.

Comparative needs can be determined by the relationship between the standards of different groups or the average for the population. In other words needs are determined with reference to some notion of equity or norm for an area or group.

These four different approaches can be complementary to each other. The need for suitable supported accommodation for a patient being discharged from a long-stay institution, for example, may be a felt need, one that is supported by professional judgements and a comparative one that determines that people in these circumstances should be enabled to live in what is considered to be a normal housing environment.

The different approaches might also conflict. The most obvious differences may be between subjective aspirations of those who consider themselves in need and the normative approach of policy makers. The former may tend towards a higher level of housing standard than those who make planning and budgetary decisions. One extreme of this is that housing of a high standard should be available for all, regardless of ability to pay. In an area of public policy such as social housing there will be inevitable party-political struggles and tensions between the perceived and expressed needs and the limited resources available to meet them. This interaction, however, can result in a dynamic definition of housing need, hotly debated at local and national levels, often mediated by professionals such as housing development officers and planners.

Meeting housing need

So far our definition of housing need can be summarized as 'the total quantity of housing that is required to provide accommodation of a given standard or above' (Barnett and Lowe 1990). This concept refers to the total stock required. However another more widely used definition 'refers to the shortfall between the actual supply of housing of at least the required standard and the quantity of housing required' (Barnett and Lowe 1990). Whereas the first definition is dependent only on the concepts of households and what is deemed acceptable standards of accommodation, this second 'deficiency concept' also depends on a third variable – *the supply of accommodation* of at least the required standard.

In using the latter definition of housing need in assessments it is necessary to take into account the means by which that supply is to be found. This definition acknowledges that in reality there will be significant constraints on the supply side. Housing, and access to it, in a mixed economy is controlled partly by the market and partly through state intervention. In a system where the state provides and allocates on the basis of criteria of need, what those criteria are will be all important. However it should not be necessary to assess housing needs in a market system that produced acceptable housing on demand, given preferences, income and wealth, although only those needs which can be afforded at market prices would be met.

However in a society that considers that relatively good standards of housing are desirable, some form of assessment and intervention will be necessary. Generally intervention in the housing market may be seen in terms of either increasing the supply of housing to an adequate level, and allocating housing in relation to meet defined need or making housing costs affordable through influencing house prices and/or incomes. It is important in this context to bear in mind that housing needs assessments should not only consider the provision of new accommodation but also involve an analysis of a range of actions which can be taken to enable households to obtain the housing they require. Policies based more on income than housing subsidies, as is currently the case, reflect political priorities and are subject to intense political debate (Arblaster and Hawtin 1993). However comprehensive local housing needs assessments should consider levels and allocation of subsidies.

As we have seen local housing needs assessments inherently take into account political influences at both the national as well as local levels. This may create problems, especially where the two have differing policy views, and therefore diverging opinions about how needs are to be measured and met.

Housing needs assessments in practice

Needs assessments are primarily of use in strategic planning and resource allocation, therefore differences in local and national assessments will reflect the differences in issues relating to their use. National housing needs assessments have been undertaken to argue the case for an additional supply of low cost rented housing to be made available at a national or regional level. Local housing needs assessments are usually undertaken by local authorities to obtain borrowing requirement to support the local strategic plan.

Assessing national housing needs

The government uses a Generalized Needs Index (GNI) to allocate capital spending consents to local authorities in England. This mechanism is currently under review along with the Housing Corporation's variant, the

Housing Needs Indicator (HNI), against which the corporation tries to ensure that allocations to housing associations respect priorities. Both use a package of needs indicators, measuring relative need to spend rather than any absolute factor. The government is currently looking at a broader approach, the New Provision Indicator, which may include the 'efficiency' of councils as one of its indicators. The GNI does not however refer to the current level of need for social rented housing.

In 1977 the Housing Policy Review established a sophisticated mechanism for assessing needs called the Medium Term Forecast. It included, for the first time, all legally accepted standards as well as some higher standards. It took into account the private market, and also improvements to existing stock. The mechanism was abandoned by the government after 1979.

Whitehead (1991) has argued that Britain has moved from a needs-based, property subsidized housing policy towards an 'affordable' approach assisting individual low-income families to obtain the housing they want in a more market oriented system. She argues that there has been an important shift in setting legal minimum standards away from 'treating housing as a merit good which should be provided because society thinks it is worthwhile, towards treating it more as a private good' (Whitehead 1991). She did, however, acknowledge that this shift may be more one of rhetoric than reality.

Since 1979 government policy has been informed by the belief that state control is fundamentally flawed, based on self-interest or ignorance, and leads to abuses of power and erosion of individual liberty. In contrast the moral superiority of the market is asserted and seen as a more efficient system for defining and meeting needs. Individual consumer power is all important and there is no basis for consensual agreement which allows the identification of collective needs. The market is seen as the correct mechanism for determining the number and type of properties necessary to meet housing need. The government therefore abandoned official forecasts of housing need, arguing that the current system for allocating housing resources was not based on an adequate measure of housing need (Shelter 1991). This argument was supported by the claim that forecasts are inevitably inaccurate, and that there was 'the largest crude surplus of houses over households that we have ever had in this country' (Secretary of State giving evidence to the Select Committee on Environment in 1981, quoted in Whitehead 1991).

Pressure groups, academic institutions and independent agencies have continued to define and assess national housing need, which took on a much higher profile in the late 1980s and early 1990s when the lack of investment in housing became even more pronounced. As assessments of housing need are largely dependent on assumptions made about the types of need to be met, for example the suitability and condition of the stock and concealed households, it is not surprising that these estimates vary. Many estimates however suggest that up to 100,000 new affordable units are needed every year during the 1990s. A number of models have been developed to quantify national housing need (Kleinman and Whitehead 1992).

The National Housing Forum (Niner 1989), the Chartered Institute of Housing (Wilcox 1989) and the Audit Commission (1992), all measured different types of national housing need through a comparison of the existing stock and forecast household growth. Kleinman and Whitehead (1992) developed a 'gross flows' approach, which assesses the number of households considered inadequately housed with reference to tenure flows within the housing stock, together with private sector investment.

Bramley (1989) also developed a model which concentrates on households unable to gain entry into owner occupation and who, it is therefore assumed, will require social provision of some kind, compared with the number of social rented dwellings available. He concluded that over half the new houses required should be in the non-metropolitan areas in the south of England, whereas only one third of new dwellings were being built there. He was heavily criticized by some who felt that problems more prevalent in the north were not reflected in his calculations. These include: the quality and conditions of much of the housing for sale and of relets (Morton 1989; Barnett and Lowe 1990).

Under such pressure the Department of the Environment produced a paper in May 1995 in which they give their estimates for 'newly arising potential *demand* for sub-market rented housing' based only on past trends and ignoring current levels of need.

Assessing local housing needs

Given increased pressure from central government, more local authorities are carrying out local housing needs surveys. In a survey of all local planning authorities in England, Wales and Scotland carried out in 1991 by Barlow and Chambers (1992) only 29 per cent stated that they had defined the local needs in their areas, and those were predominantly in rural areas. Two years later Barlow *et al.* (1994) found that of the authorities who have an affordable housing policy, 45 per cent had established a definition of 'housing need'.

A number of guides to local housing needs assessments have been produced over the last two decades, few of which attempt to provide an ideal model. As van Zijl (1993) states 'the standardisation of housing needs assessments is neither a feasible nor a desirable option'. Each authority, and each assessment, will have different aims, values and circumstances. Van Zijl, however, suggests that the government should produce guidelines to allow a degree of conformity to ensure a consistently high standard and to enable comparisons to be made. The handbooks which have been produced provide guidance about the range of issues, information sources and methods authorities should be aware of and that might be appropriate to their areas and type of authority.[1]

Methodologies for local housing needs assessments

The process of assessing housing needs includes: defining the concept of housing need; translating national economic conditions into a local context; analysing current housing demand (disaggregated by categories such as special need, women and ethnic minority communities) and supply of all tenures; producing three to 10-year projections of need; matching the existing stock to tenants' needs; and, with an understanding of the availability of resources, evaluating a broad set of options to identify solutions to the problems described. This is a complex practice and raises a number of key issues.

The basis of most quantitative housing needs assessments is a calculation of the demand for housing compared to its supply, usually related to the public sector, although it increasingly applies to all sectors. The first stage is to esti-mate the number of separate, and potentially separate, households. Con-cealed, or hidden, households are more difficult to estimate, and once an estimate has been made there is the difficulty of determining the percentage of hidden households that actually want a separate dwelling.

The next stage is to project the number of households that are likely to exist in the future. This again can be problematic. Population forecasts, based on past trends, can be made but the formation of households does not necessarily reflect this trend. The number of households since World War II, for example, has grown significantly faster than the population growth, with a fall in average household size from 2.89 in 1971 to 2.48 in 1991.

Once the total number of households has been established, the supply of housing is calculated. The number of houses available can be disaggregated by tenure, size, type, location and so on. Some houses are likely to become obso-lete over the timescale of the projected assessment and need to be deducted from the total stock. The total supply is then subtracted from the total number of households, plus a vacancy factor to allow for mobility, to give a crude surplus or shortage. If a deficiency needs assessment is to be made the likely level of new building will need to be estimated in one or more of the housing sectors. As the local authority will no longer be the residual supplier, options for alternative providers will need to be explored. The supply of accommo-dation, given sufficient quantities and all else being equal, can create a demand. Therefore when considering housing supply it must be recognized that it is likely to reduce demand by less than the quantity supplied.

When this comparison of the total number of households with the number of dwellings has been attempted, on both a local as well as national scale, there can appear to be a gross surplus of dwellings, as occurred nationally in the early 1970s, from which it may be inferred there is no real housing need. However, a situation in which there are more empty properties than people who are homeless may not indicate an absence of need. Indeed the existence of people without adequate accommodation could, itself, be taken as evidence of need. The specific requirements for tenure, size, type of accommodation and afford-ability need to be considered; an area with a high proportion of owner occu-pied housing, for example, may not be able to meet the needs of people unable or unwilling to buy. Homelessness alongside a crude housing surplus can rep-resent an incompatibility between market forces and public policies. Housing needs assessments must take account of both the market conditions in the private sector and allocations and eligibility policies in the social sector.

Waiting lists

A systematic calculation of housing shortage, especially involving residents surveys, can be costly and time consuming. Therefore analysis of local authority waiting lists have played an important role in assessments of housing needs, a practice encouraged in the past by government guidance (SDD 1977; DoE 1980). More recently the Audit Commission (1992) has stated that 'a properly maintained waiting list is still a major source of information on local housing needs'. Up-to-date waiting lists can give an indication of trends in demand from particular household types or sizes, or in the pattern of offers and refusals, and can be useful as a secondary source of information.

However, the use of waiting lists as a reliable technique for comprehensive needs assessment has been heavily criticized. The DoE review *Routes into Local Authority Housing* (1994), found that despite growing evidence of list review procedures, 'waiting lists were poor indicators of housing need with only 43% of applicants still living at the registered address, and wanting housing now, a percentage virtually unchanged since 1986'. They also found that one in 10 had registered as an 'insurance policy' in case they might require housing in the future. Conversely, Shelter found that 61 per cent of people who approached their advice centres and were lacking secure accommodation were not registered on a local authority housing waiting list. Preoccupation with waiting lists assumes that the authority is only concerned with those who apply for and are eligible for council housing. The needs of those who do not apply because they do not want that form of tenure, or because they do not think they will qualify, are effectively ignored.

Special needs

The needs of specific groups in the population, such as elderly people, people with mental or physical disabilities, people with learning difficulties, people who are homeless, and people in need of supported accommodation, are often addressed in either a separate section of the assessment or by studies which focus primarily on one group.[2] Special needs are now being assessed more extensively by housing authorities to assist in the formulation of community care plans. Watson and Harker (1993) have developed a 'housing pathways' model of housing needs assessments, with reference to people with learning disabilities, designed to produce a five-year forecast of the need for supported housing in the social rented sector. The model is based on an analysis of people's living circumstances and the factors triggering moves between different types of accommodation. In their study they found that assessments can be complicated by a number of factors:

- The housing demands of the majority of people needing care services are filtered through other care agencies.
- Much of the demand remains unexpressed.
- There is a wide range of groups of residents and types and forms of supported housing which makes prioritization difficult.
- Housing needs may be seen differently by the various agencies involved in setting priorities and distributing resources.
- The users of care, their carers and professionals may have widely differing views on the types of accommodation needed.

(Watson and Harker 1993)

Sources of information

There is potentially a vast amount of information that could be collected, stored and used as part of a housing needs assessment. Depending on the aims and approach of the assessment this might include current and projected information on: inward and outward migrations; emerging households; household size and composition; categories of concealed households; employment, income and travel to work patterns; and individual preferences, attitudes and aspirations in relation to factors such as house type and tenure (including shared ownership); distance from workplace; access; and affordability, rent levels and house prices.

Some possible sources of secondary information include: the Census of Population; demographic projections; records (such as waiting lists, transfer applications, allocations, and homelessness applications); tenant feedback forms; reports (for example stating existing policies, or concerning homelessness); grant application forms and planning controls; hospital closure lists; and existing surveys such as parish council area profiles.

Primary information can be obtained through a stock condition survey, a residents survey and through interviews with representatives of key agencies and organizations such as: estate agents and building societies; housing associations; health authorities; social services departments; Women's Aid; Shelter; residents' groups; parish councils and so on.

House condition surveys at a national level provide only very general indications of conditions and trends. Local surveys are therefore necessary to provide detailed information about disrepair and deficiencies in different house types and tenures. The tendency has been for local authorities to rely on small scale surveys, on information which is unsystematic and may be out-of-date. Such information may be simply based on local officers' *ad hoc* knowledge or assumptions (such as that the older stock, or system built properties, are in the worst condition). If a customer centred approach is to be adopted, household surveys should be an integral aspect of assessment, and if conducted alongside a stock condition survey will help explain and identify many of the causes of poor conditions.

Issues

It is important that parameters for a housing needs assessment are agreed at the outset. Two of the more important ones are the timescale of any projected forecasts and the indicators of housing need to be used. Cullingworth (1979) reminds us that 'The assessment of need would be only a snapshot picture of an essentially dynamic situation'. Housing needs assessments are primarily based on statistics relating to one point in time. Housing is a durable commodity, however, and there are considerable time lags in the construction process. Therefore housing strategies should cover a three-year period at least and the local plans of authorities for a 10-year period. Any forecasts of needs that are made are likely to require revision during the planning period.

An initial overview of the main social and economic characteristics of the designated area is important in helping to place the assessment in context and to explain some of the findings. This could include identification of areas of high or low need (a surplus of housing may not be sufficient to meet requirements if it is in an area of low need), and the health of the local economy (including economic growth and its distribution, unemployment, income levels and inflation). An understanding of the housing market is also important. Housing needs assessments are beginning to recognize that the housing market is not homogeneous and that it is necessary to be sensitive to the variations in housing characteristics and needs of housing in all sectors. There is a paucity of readily understandable and proven methods for reliably estimating demand for housing across all sectors. Goodlad (1993) feels that this is partly due to the intrinsic difficulty of developing planning techniques for a complex commodity such as housing, affected as it is by the tax system, the local planning context and unique local social geographies.

An understanding of the resources that are available for housing are a key aspect of the assessment. Resources may include the land bank available and its zoning situation, administrative resources available to the local authority, planning agreement potential, data concerning the construction industry, activities and intentions of housing associations and the authority's own spending power.

There are also issues that particularly affect rural authorities. Many of these have been addressed in Rural Voice's *Meeting Rural Housing Need* (1994) and ACRE's *Enabling Rural Social Housing* (1993). They relate to the definition of the boundaries of the assessment (within a village, parish or wider) and the size of many rural areas which mean that sample surveys would not produce accurate enough results.

Applications

General applications

Housing needs assessments are not an end in themselves; they are a valuable tool that can serve a variety of functions. The principal ones are as follows:

- to provide an information base from which an authority, in its role as enabler, can plan its policies, develop a strategy and identify priorities for action;
- to facilitate the effective selection of priority areas for new initiatives and developments to inform planning policies;
- to provide a baseline against which to monitor subsequent developments;
- to provide a context for an authority's strategic aims and day to day decisions;
- to provide a vehicle for better coordination and systematic sharing of information between local departments and other interested agencies and organizations;
- to involve residents and staff in, for example, developing a new initiative or forming a bid for Estate Action;
- to act as a bargaining/advocacy document to support the case for housing investment through the identification of areas of housing need and the

securing of the commitment of other agencies who may be involved in the implementation of the strategy;
* to help raise the national profile of housing by highlighting local and national housing need.

The impact of housing needs assessments

The government has made it increasingly clear that the future success of local authorities' capital allocation proposals will depend on the identification of housing needs and the involvement of residents in formulating appropriate housing strategies. Many local authorities are undertaking local housing needs assessments which are having a considerable impact on the distribution of scarce resources which are being targeted on people and property most in need.

Local authorities, however, now have significantly less control over the provision of low cost rented accommodation and are having to seek alternative means of enabling affordable housing such as partnership and land deals with housing associations. Another mechanism is the use of planning agreements between local authorities and private developers (Barlow *et al.* 1994). Local authorities, largely in rural areas, are managing to secure a 'quota' of affordable housing on larger development sites. The government's Planning Policy Guidance Note 3 (PPG3) states that such a quota can be secured where there is 'demonstrable lack of affordable housing to meet local needs'. As a result many planning authorities are now undertaking local housing needs assessments, resulting in the provision of low cost rented accommodation in areas that might not otherwise have benefited.

All local authorities are required to make provision for housing in Unitary Development Plans and Local Plans. Local housing needs assessments are also an important element of bids for funding such as Housing Renewal Areas and the Estate Action element of the Single Regeneration Budget. Worthwhile renewal strategies require detailed mapping of social, economic and physical characteristics including housing needs. Local authorities are beginning to understand that stock condition surveys, linked with resident perception surveys, can have a significant impact on decisions about spending.

Housing authorities are increasingly working with other local authority departments and organizations to assess housing need in their area, such as with social services over community care plans, planning departments over the development of affordable housing policies, and with housing associations over the needs of special groups in the community. Councils are having to adopt a more corporate approach to preparing strategies which accords with the greater integration of housing and planning functions as outlined in PPG3.

Experience from decentralized authorities and from work on 'priority estates' shows that an increased awareness of local needs greatly enhances service delivery. In 1989 legislation was passed enforcing housing authorities to publish performance indicators in relation to housing management. Many authorities developed their collection and analysis of needs information to provide a context for these indicators. Local authorities in some areas are also currently undertaking needs and opinion surveys to inform tender specifications in relation to compulsory competitive tendering of housing management functions or in preparation for the transfer of their stock. Such assessments should significantly enhance the quality of service delivery to tenants.

Conclusions

Local housing needs assessments have developed over the last 60 years and have grown out of the responsibility of the state to respond to the housing needs of its citizens. Until 1979 it was commonly understood that the role of a local authority was to define the need for low cost housing in its area, and to provide for any unmet needs by building and managing appropriate properties. However formal assessments of housing need were rarely undertaken.

The current system of national housing resources allocation adopts a narrow definition of housing. The HIP submission is heavily biased towards the view that housing is simply shelter and does not take into account, for example, tenant insecurity or the quality of the neighbourhood. Questions about how to define 'adequate accommodation', what constitutes a 'household' and how needs are met all involve subjective judgements and are, in part, politically determined. Differing perspectives on these issues between national and local government make effective local housing needs assessments even more problematic.

In undertaking a local housing needs assessment, a local authority is faced with a range of different approaches and methods from which to choose. Such assessments can be complex and may stretch the limited resources available. There are also issues relating to the quality of the information available and the technical expertise which may be required in collecting and analysing the data.

However a comprehensive, systematic assessment of local housing needs can provide information of use in decision making about the allocation of scarce resources and can result in practical assistance to those most in need.

Notes

1 Further information on local housing needs assessments can be obtained from the following: Scottish Development Department (1977) *Assessing Housing Need: A Manual of Guidance*; DoE (1980) *Housing Requirements: A Guide to Information and Techniques*; Audit Commission (1992) *Developing Local Authority Housing Strategies*; Parker (1993) *Taking Stock: A Guide to Local Housing Assessment*; and van Zijl (1993) *A Guide to Local Housing Needs Assessment*.

  For further details about housing needs surveys consult: London Research Centre (1986) *The Housing Needs Survey: A Comprehensive Method of Assessing Housing Requirements*; or the Joint Centre for Survey Methods Newsletter which reported on the ESRC Survey Methods Seminar in 1992 on Methodology of Housing Surveys (Joint Centre for Survey Methods 1992).

2 Examples of local or national studies carried out to assess the housing needs of particular groups include; single people (Brady *et al.* 1991); those with HIV or Aids (HIV Aids and Housing Project undated); women escaping violence (Charles

1994); people with physical disabilities (Disabled Persons Accommodation Agency 1995); and people with special needs (Office for Public Management 1992).

References

ACRE (1993) *Enabling Rural Social Housing.* Cirencester: ACRE.

Arblaster, L. and Hawtin, M. (1993) *Health, Housing and Social Policy.* London: Socialist Health Association.

Archbishop of Canterbury Commission on Urban Poverty Areas (1985) *Faith in the City. Report by the Archbishop of Canterbury Commission on Urban Poverty Areas.* London: Church House Publishing.

Association of Metropolitan Authorities (AMA) (1987) *Local Housing Strategies.* London: AMA.

Audit Commission (1992) *Developing Local Authority Housing Strategies.* London: HMSO.

Barlow, J. and Chambers, D. (1992) *Planning Agreements and Social Housing Quotas.* York: Joseph Rowntree Foundation.

Barlow, J., Cocks, R. and Parker, M. (1994) *Planning for Affordable Housing.* London: Department of the Environment.

Barnett, P.R. and Lowe, S. (1990) Measuring housing need and the provision of social housing, *Housing Studies,* 5: 184–94.

Bradshaw, J. (1972) A taxonomy of social need. In G. McLachan (ed.) *Problems and Progress in Medical Care.* Seventh series, Oxford: Oxford University Press.

Brady, S., Cutter, J., Percy-Smith, J., Rowetz, A. and Wraight, M. (1991) *The Housing Needs of Single People in Harrogate.* Leeds: Policy Research Unit.

Bramley, G. (1989) *Meeting Housing Needs.* London: Association of District Councils.

Bramley, G. (1990) *Bridging the Affordability Gap.* Birmingham: BEC Publications.

Central Housing Advisory Committee (1969) *Council Housing Purposes, Procedures and Priorities.* London: HMSO.

Charles, N. (1994) The housing needs of women and children escaping domestic violence. *Journal of Social Policy,* 23(4): 465–87.

Cole, I. and Goodchild, B. (1995) Local housing strategies in England; An assessment of their changing role and content, *Policy and Politics,* 23(1): 52.

Cullingworth, J.B. (1979) *Essays on housing policy: The British scene.* London: George Allen and Unwin.

Department of the Environment (DoE) (1977) *Housing Policy: A Consultative Document.* Cmnd 6851, London: HMSO.

Department of the Environment (DoE) (1980) *Housing Requirements: A Guide to Information and Techniques.* London: HMSO.

Department of the Environment (DoE) (1987) *Housing: The Government's Proposals.* Cmnd 214, London: HMSO.

Department of the Environment (DoE) (1995) *Provision for Social Housing – Background Analysis.* London: DoE.

Disabled Persons Accommodation Agency (DPAA) (1995) *Housing Needs of People with Physical Disabilities.* Housing Research Findings 136, York: Joseph Rowntree Foundation.

Doyal, L. and Gough, I. (1991) *A Theory of Human Need.* London: Macmillan.

Goodlad, R. (1993) *The Housing Authority as Enabler.* Coventry/Essex: Longman and Institute of Housing.

HIV Aids and Housing Project (undated) *Addressing Local Housing Needs for People with HIV.* London: HIV Aids and Housing Project.

Hoyle, W. and Brindley, T. (1983) Housing strategies in practice – Problems and opportunities, *Local Government Studies*, May/June: 31–44.

Joint Centre for Survey Methods Newsletter (1992) *Methodology of Housing Surveys*, 12(1), London: Social and Community Planning Research and the London School of Economics and Political Science.

Labour Party National Executive Committee (NEC) (1985) *Home for the Future; A Statement to the Labour Annual Conference 1985*. London: The Labour Party.

London Research Centre (1986) *The Housing Needs Survey: A Comprehensive Method of Assessing Housing Requirements*. London: London Research Centre.

Malpass, P. and Murie, A. (1994) *Housing Policy and Practice*, 4th edn. Basingstoke: Macmillan.

Mellinger, L. (1994) Housing the community, *Cities*, 11(2): 95–106.

Merrett, S. (1986) *Local Housing Plans*. London: Haringey Council.

Morris, J. (1980) The rise and fall of local housing strategies, *Housing Review*, 6, May: 50–3.

Morton, J. (1989) The North/South Divide: Whose need is the greatest? *Housing*, June: 16–19.

Niner, P. (1989) *Housing needs in the 1990s: An interim assessment*. London: National Housing Forum.

Office for Public Management (1992) *Assessment of the Housing Requirements of People with Special Needs Over the Next Decade*. London: National Federation of Housing Associations.

Parker, J. (1993) *Taking Stock: A Guide to Local Housing Assessment*. Cardiff: Housing Management Advisory Panel.

Rural Voice (1994) *Meeting Rural Housing Need*. Cirencester: Rural Voice.

Scottish Development Department (SDD) (1977) *Scottish Housing Handbook 1: Assessing Housing Need – A Manual of Guidance*. Glasgow: Scottish Development Department.

Seebohm Report (1968) *Report of the Committee on Local Authority and Allied Personal Social Services*. London: HMSO.

Shelter (1991) *Moving Forward: A Programme to Meet Housing Need*. London: Shelter.

Singh, M. (1994) Back door, *Roof*, March/April: 44.

Watson, L. and Harker, M. (1993) *Community Care Planning: A Model for Housing Needs Assessment*. London: Institute of Housing and National Federation of Housing Associations.

Whitehead, C. (1991) From need to affordability: An analysis of UK housing objectives, *Urban Studies*, 28(6): 871–87.

Whitehead, C. and Kleinman, M. (1992) *A Review of Housing Needs Assessments*. London: Housing Corporation.

Wilcox, S. (1989) *The Need for Social Rented Housing in England in the 1990s*. Coventry: Chartered Institute of Housing.

van Zijl, V. (1993) *A Guide to Local Housing Needs Assessment*. Coventry: Institute of Housing.

ASSESSING NEEDS FOR LEGAL SERVICES

Introduction

This chapter details the methodology and preliminary results of a current project being undertaken by the Legal Aid Board which attempts to use needs analysis and cartography as a tool to assist the Board in implementing its strategy on access to legal services. First the concept of need in relation to legal services will be examined. Next this will be further developed by looking at the related concept of access to legal services. A methodology for measuring likely need for legal services is then presented and its possible applications considered.

The concept of need for legal services

The Legal Aid Board is a non-departmental public body created under the Legal Aid Act 1988. It took over responsibility for the administration of legal aid from the Law Society, the professional body for solicitors in England and Wales, which had been administering the system since 1949. In 1994/5 it was responsible for the administration of legal aid net payments to lawyers of just in excess of £1 billion. There has been increasing concern about the cost of legal aid. During 1981–91 the annual net growth of the Legal Aid Fund was more than three times the rate of inflation and twice the rate of growth of the GDP over the same period. At the same time concern has been expressed by Baldwin and Hill (1988: 105), Kempson (1989: 71) and Abel (1988: 231) about the narrowness of the provision of legal assistance, with the bulk of work of most private practice solicitors remaining within the traditional areas of conveyancing, crime, matrimonial and wills. The area of social welfare law has been largely untouched by private practice. Housing, immigration, social security and employment law are some examples. The Lord Chancellor's Advisory Committee on Legal Aid has raised this issue on a number of occasions, commenting that: 'The mere existence of solicitors is not enough to guarantee that they will be meeting the legal needs of the areas in which they are situated' (*36th Annual Reports of the Law Society and the Lord Chancellor's Advisory Committee* 1985–6: para. 93).

It has been left to the advice sector to become what Abel has termed part of the 'collective producers' (1988: 298–302) of legal services in those areas of law, mainly without any support from legal aid funds. The mixed nature of funding for these agencies has given rise to an *ad hoc* and geographically uneven distribution of services. The extent to which legal services are provided also varies, as does the scope of the service. The concept of need for legal services that are financed from the legal aid fund has been determined substantially by the services that are offered by the private suppliers – solicitors. These are the legal services that they have traditionally supplied and been trained in. In a rare exploration of access to legal services in a rural context, the Exeter team working on Access to Justice in Rural Britain concluded that:

> reliance on traditional forms of delivery through the private professions was unlikely to provide either the scope of service or the specific legal specialisms demanded by the poor and otherwise disadvantaged groups in rural areas.
>
> (Economides and Blacksell 1987: 364)

The Access Committee of the Legal Aid Board concluded that an analysis of actual legal needs was required across a broader spectrum of legal topics, rather than having total reliance on the needs as perceived by the main suppliers of the service. At a policy level this, as well as attempts to curb the growth of the legal aid budget, have led to a re-examination of the role of publicly funded legal provision and the priority of the various demands made upon that budget (Legal Action Group 1992). The Legal Aid Board is a major participant in this debate because it has statutory functions that relate to the issue of access to legal services. These are closely linked to the purpose of the Legal Aid Act 1988 which is to:

> establish a framework for the provision . . . of advice, assistance and representation which is publicly funded with a view to helping persons who might otherwise be unable to obtain advice, assistance or representation on account of their means.
>
> (section 1)

The Board has very wide powers under the Act to assist in the establishment of a framework for the provision of publicly funded legal services. These include the power to do:

> anything – (a) which it considers necessary or desirable to provide or ensure the provision of advice, assistance and representation . . . and advice, assistance and representation may be provided in different ways in different areas of England and Wales and in different ways in different fields of law.
>
> (section 4(1))

This power would enable regional priorities to be satisfied if there was a mechanism whereby different regional needs could be identified. This is the statutory authority for the proposals in the Green Paper on legal aid for the development of regional boards to advise the Legal Aid Board on priorities for expenditure (Lord Chancellor's Department 1995). The boards would use the needs analysis models described in this chapter as one indicator to guide decisions.

The Board was further encouraged to move in this direction in July 1988 when guidance was provided by the Lord Chancellor. He stated that, within the framework of the Act

> the Board's overall aim should be to ensure that legal advice, assistance and representation is made available to those who need it. It should be provided in ways which are effective and give the best possible value for money.
>
> (Legal Aid Board 1989: para. 2)

The Board was confronted with the considerable practical difficulty of trying to implement and monitor this ambitious objective. There was also a related requirement to assess the quality of the legal services that were being provided as part of the issue of access to legal services. The Lord Chancellor's introduction to the White Paper in July 1987 stated:

> [I]n legal services, there should be the widest range of choice, compatible with the maintenance of standards, available both from lawyers and from other appropriate specialists, and with enough information and client safeguards to make that choice a real one . . . The government's overall aim is to improve access to good quality legal services, to the courts and ultimately to justice.
>
> (Lord Chancellor's Department 1987: 4)

The Board had already taken some steps towards the development of a quality framework for publicly funded legal providers as mentioned in the Act and by the Lord Chancellor. This policy development was proceeding under the title of 'Franchising', which is an attempt to develop consistent standards of delivery of legal aid services that can be monitored, the Board working in partnership with franchisees (Blake and Orchard 1989, 1990; Legal Aid Board 1992, 1993; Blake 1993). A consistent service to an agreed standard in the relevant area of law must be embraced in any definition of access to legal services (Kempson 1989: 66–7). But what is the definition of access to legal services? How can it be measured to assess whether policies are improving or denying access? What structures are needed to monitor, promote and improve access? These are the issues that confronted the Board and led to the decision to attempt to establish a model that provides some indication of the relative need for legal services in different areas of law and in different locations. This was a crucial component in assessing the extent to which access to legal services is provided.

Some research had already been undertaken on the current usage of the Advice and Assistance scheme within the legal aid framework. This scheme is known as the Green Form scheme because of the colour of the form that solicitors have to complete (Baldwin and Hill 1988; Kempson 1989). However this research was mainly based on interviews with, and questionnaires completed by, the providers of legal services: solicitors and advice agencies. There had been no analysis of nationally available data to assess whether it could be used to provide an indicator of the need for different types of legal services. If such a model was possible then it could be used as one of a number of tools to assist in policy development in the prioritization of scarce resources, the promotion of innovative methods of delivery, and the opening up of legal aid funding to other providers of legal services, not just by solicitors in private practice. It could also open up an opportunity for greater diversity according to regional needs.

Targeting needs and access to legal services

Needs analysis is not a phrase that is commonly used with regard to the provision of legal services. 'Access', either to justice or legal services, is a phrase that is more common. However, this is rarely defined and, with the exception of the Access to Justice in Rural Britain Project (Economides and Blacksell 1987), the methods through which 'access' can be monitored and pursued are rarely discussed. Access implies an assessment of the supply of legal services as well as the need for them. There have been some attempts to quantify the extent of the need for financial legal services and the access that individuals have to specialist services in this area, but this work has not been extrapolated through the use of national data sets to provide a global perspective that can be used to monitor a changing situation (Hinton and Berthoud 1988; Berthoud and Kempson 1992). However this work does provide an invaluable guide to the key features that affect the presence of legal need; these can be used as building blocks for the development of a model that attempts to assess legal need.

The requirement for such a model is not just driven by current resource and policy requirements. There is an important historical context relating to the identification of the need for legal services and the making of assessments as to whether that need is being met. This can be observed in an analysis of the development of legal aid. Despite the constant criticisms from the profession concerning the rates of legal aid remuneration, the Legal Aid and Advice Act 1949 still needs to be recognized as the enactment that led legal aid away from its charitable past. In the medieval period poor people relied on principles of Christian charity and even chivalry to seek redress before the courts. The *in forma pauperis* procedure of 1495 required a judge to assign counsel without payment. This procedure lasted until the nineteenth century. Its charitable nature was underlined by members of the judiciary who, without statutory authority, even sanctioned the flogging of those who received aid but lost their case (Cappelletti *et al.* 1975; Cappelletti and Gordley 1977: 347). In the late eighteenth century in France and the United States, and the late nineteenth century in the United Kingdom, the state started to see that it was part of its function to guarantee a right to a lawyer. Out of the French and American revolutions evolved a principle of justice based upon the preservation of citizens' rights through equality before the law, and the power of the individual within society from which some theories of sovereign power are derived. However, these revolutionary reforms were incomplete because 'lawyers still demanded fees that the poor could not pay' (Cappelletti and Gordley 1977: 355).

This was a real 'access' problem. There was a gap between the constitutional guarantee of access to the law and the inability of individuals to gain access because there was no state scheme for financing the implementation of that guarantee. The state relied on the charity of lawyers to fill the gap, but this was not a solution to the problems of the poor or the pursuit of actual equality as opposed to formal equality. In the United Kingdom the proposals in the Report of the Committee on Legal Aid and Legal Advice in England and Wales (Rushcliffe Committee 1945) gave rise to the Act of 1949 which was a step towards the state filling this gap. It can be seen that the provision of a right to a lawyer may resolve the problem of formal equality but it does little to assist in the promotion of actual equality. It is this gap between formal and actual equality that provides the historical context and justification for the pursuit of a model that can provide indicators of legal need. The franchising initiative is also an attempt to fill this gap. Actual as opposed to formal access can be denied because of a shortfall in the quality of the delivery of the service. An example of this shortfall has been identified in the police station duty solicitor scheme. This scheme was established under the Police and Criminal Evidence Act 1984 (sections 58, 59) and provides for a statutory right of access to a lawyer, 100 per cent eligibility (i.e. no means test) and nearly national availability through the establishment of a duty solicitor structure administered by the Board (Blake *et al.* 1988). Research carried out for the Lord Chancellor's Department showed that there was a poor standard of service being provided under the scheme by solicitors and their clerks (Sanders *et al.* 1989). Research for the Board illustrated that this poor standard-also applied to detainees in police stations who had requested to see their own solicitor rather than the duty solicitor (Hodgson 1991).

Therefore any definition of access to legal services needs to incorporate the distinction between the formal and actual situations and must include all the factors which could affect access, including quality. The Board have set out their definition as follows: 'Access is achieved where individuals are aware of their need for legal services and can select and actually obtain legal services of an appropriate quality, at a price within reach' (Legal Aid Board 1990–1: 24).

The assessment of need for legal services is only one of the indicators that will assist in the policy development of publicly funded legal services. There are other factors to be considered in developing an effective access policy: awareness of legal rights and remedies, the availability of services that can help, the quality of the services that are available and affordability. But a model that can contribute data on needs assessment is a key component in the wider assessment of access to legal services.

Measuring the need for legal services

The model that the Board has developed attempts to provide data that can assist in the measurement and monitoring of part of the definition of access to legal services. Indicators that measure relative need for legal services in particular fields of law would assist the ability to measure the effect that policies have on access and to target and prioritize the fields of law in particular locations that need attention. Prioritizing the allocation of legal aid resources would focus attention on those fields of law and geographical areas where access is poor. Different areas have different priorities and the need for this to be reflected in policy development is supported by the research undertaken by Kempson into the Green Form scheme (1989: 71–4). This type of approach has also been developed and justified by Jarman with regard to the provision of medical services:

> It is often said that we know where the worst areas are and that it is a waste of time and resources trying to define them more accurately; and in any case attempts at quantitative analysis are bound to fail. If, however, it is eventually decided for instance that action will be taken which will have different financial consequences for those working inside and outside underprivileged areas it will be necessary to justify the reason for choosing certain areas and to be able precisely to specify how each was defined.
>
> (1983: 1705; Jarman 1984)

With these objectives in mind the Board has developed statistical models that assist in the identification of priority areas for access to legal services. The models are portrayed in colour maps which have been published in the Board's Annual Report (Legal Aid Board 1991–2: 26–33). This reflects the view asserted by Economides and Blacksell that 'cartography and human geography hold considerable potential to redirect both the theory and practice of law' (1987: 354).

The first models provided indicators of the need for legal services in the areas of housing and debt (Legal Aid Board 1991: 26–33). This has now been extended to cover welfare benefits and immigration/nationality and continued development work is seen as a 'high priority' (Legal Aid Board 1994: 30–1). The indicators are not intended to predict the number of households or individuals in need but are a means of providing a relative index of need allowing comparisons between regions to be made. Because this information is intended to be used to feed into regional assessments of priorities on a national basis, the model had to be based on nationally available statistics.

The North Western Legal Services Committee (NWLSC) assisted in testing the accuracy of the model, which involved putting the findings up against the qualitative perceptions of a wide range of people working in the field in Oldham, Derby and, on a much wider scale, Lancashire. There was an initial literature search to ascertain the principal factors that had been assessed as influencing the need for legal assistance in the areas of housing and debt. Using these factors, the Access Committee of the Board developed a statistical model based on nationally available information that was, or could be, available in a postcode format. However the process started with information that was initially based on wards, principally the small area census data. The model was tested in two towns, Oldham and Derby. The qualitative testing involved a meeting of individuals who were aware of the problems in the towns. This included the police, advice workers, lawyers, community workers, representatives of the local authority and, in one instance, a vicar. The meetings were informed of the purpose of the exercise and, in small groups, were asked to rank the wards in order of need priority in both housing and debt. Maps were provided. The groups then came together and debated an agreed ranking of the wards for housing and debt. The meetings were then introduced to the ranking that the model provided and discussed the degree of difference and possible reasons. The main differences arose from the changes in the local authority rented sector since the 1981 census; whole housing estates had disappeared. The amount of rented housing is one of the major components in the model and the local representatives confirmed the inclusion of this parameter by prioritizing the new areas of rented provision that the old census figures did not reflect. One other difference was the increased weighting that the groups gave to concentrations of the ethnic minority population. The amended model was altered to incorporate some of the differences. On some occasions the groups' perception of the distribution of unemployment in wards was incorrect although they did consider unemployment to be an important factor.

Another meeting took place in Preston to discuss the application of the model over a wider geographical area. The purpose of the meeting was to test the validity of the amended model and to assess whether or not it was possible for a group of individuals with detailed knowledge about the provision of legal services in the area to use the information, with their local knowledge, to arrive at a consensus view about the priorities in the region. The 'region' for this meeting was Lancashire. The model was still using 1981 census figures which affected the accuracy. The meeting split into different regions within Lancashire, composition of the groups being dependent upon the individual's knowledge of that region.

The model was seen by the meeting as being a fairly accurate indicator of legal need. The main discrepancies between the model and the group perception of the actual situation again related to changes in the rented sector not being reflected in the 1981 census and some local situations which the model could not pick up. The meeting continued to prioritize the geographical location of the primary and substantial needs in housing and debt using the information and their local knowledge. One representative from a local authority which operated a social security advice service indicated that it would affect his decision making in respect of the allocation of local authority resources.

This testing confirmed that it is vital to have local input into the development of what are in effect regional strategies for tackling the problems of identifying needs and the means of satisfying them. This local input is needed in order:

- to ensure that the model's results are not being distorted by some local phenomena that will be known locally. An example is the amount of rented accommodation in an area used for holiday lettings. The model cannot detect this but the amount of rented accommodation is a factor in determining housing need. It became clear that this was distorting the figures in the Fylde area of Blackpool and in Southport;

- to reach agreement on the priorities in the region, developing a local consensus on the main issues that need to be tackled. The consensus may not be easy to achieve, but the objective data does assist in helping to overcome local competition within the region for funding, focusing discussion on the areas of greatest need; and
- to assess the resources that can be marshalled to tackle the priority areas. Although most publicly funded legal services obtain their funding from the legal aid fund, there are other sources of funding, the main one being local authority support for advice agencies and Law Centres. This is detailed knowledge about the availability of legal resources outside of the legal aid framework which is only available at a regional level. A local consensus could lead to joint funding programmes and a more focused approach in the use of all resources to tackle the accepted priorities.

The needs assessment models

The housing and debt models are both based on nationally available statistics including the 1991 census, unemployment figures from the Department of Employment and County Court Judgements from the Lord Chancellor's Department. The models are applied to postal sectors (sub-areas, e.g. OL 21) within postal areas. Postal sectors are not uniform in geographical size but contain an average of 2500 households.

The models provided indicators of needs for legal services in the areas of housing and debt. These two areas of law were chosen following a series of visits by the Access Committee of the Board throughout England and Wales which resulted in the identification of these two areas as clear priorities for action. It was also felt that the housing needs analysis could be a building block for any other legal needs analysis, a factor that was supported in the meetings which were held to discuss the models.

Applications

A possible structure that could implement the policy on a regional basis and use the information provided by the models has been considered. The NWLSC has been a valuable experiment since 1977. It was the first attempt to develop regional panels of lawyers and non-lawyers to encourage and motivate methods of delivering access to legal services and to monitor local provision. The then Lord Chancellor suggested that lay people should play a greater role in the administration of publicly funded legal services. The Legal Aid Committee of the Law Society asked the North Western Legal Aid Area Committee to establish the first Legal Services Committee so as to gain experience of how such a committee might operate. Part of the intention was that there should be close links between such committees and the Legal Aid Area Office, but in practice this did not occur. The Royal Commission on Legal Services in 1979 raised hopes that there would be a national structure of such committees, but this never materialized. The NWLSC covered Greater Manchester originally, but in 1982, operating under a new constitution and a new name it expanded to cover Lancashire and Cumbria. However it was not until recently that there have been clearer links into the development of legal aid strategy. The Lord Chancellor resisted efforts to include the establishment of Legal Services Committees in the Legal Aid Act 1988, but left it open for the Board to set them up if they saw fit (*Hansard* 4.7.88, col. 1231). The Board has the power to do so under the Legal Aid Act 1988, Schedule 1, para. 11(3).

The Board has now agreed to a new remit for the NWLSC to implement the Board's strategy in relation to the assessment and monitoring of access to legal services. A pilot scheme started in October 1992, the NWLSC having the remit to assess regional priorities for the provision of legal services using the models, to propose access targets, to develop a regional strategy for meeting those targets and to monitor the implementation of that strategy. The NWLSC will liaise with the Board and other agencies over the action that can be taken. This could include the development of different methods of delivery on an experimental basis. There is a new reporting structure, providing the NWLSC with an opportunity to influence the development of legal aid policy by providing advice to the Board based on a regional assessment of the access priorities and the different methods of tackling those priorities. A member of the Board now chairs the Committee. If successful, this structure could provide a mechanism for evolving regional strategies on a national basis (Legal Action Group 1992: 131). The next step, devolution of fixed budgets to meet the varying needs, would be logical. This would provide a structure for assessing need and planning how to move towards meeting that need, rather than just allowing the legal profession to determine the objectives for legal aid and its provision through the work that they do and always have done.

The Green Paper on the development of legal aid strategy confirms this approach, which is not surprising given all the preparatory work that has been undertaken since 1988. It suggests an extension of the NWLSC concept more closely allied to the legal aid area offices, and with clear responsibilities for advising on regional priorities (Lord Chancellor's Department 1995: para. 5.17). This is why it was important to start to develop some indicators of need based on nationally available statistics to provide an indicator for those who are making the decisions on spending priorities.

This inevitably leads to some form of planning to overcome the inadequacies of the private practice supplier approach. Alan Paterson, in an unpublished report commissioned on the financing of legal services by the Scottish Department in 1987, commented that:

> With the increasing importance of cost, effectiveness, efficiency, accountability and quality in relation to state funded legal services, a strong case exists for greater planning by the independent Boards and Commissions responsible for legal aid. A first step in the United Kingdom would be to study the cost-effectiveness and quality of the existing judicare and

salaried programmes. Another would be to produce area plans for the most efficient allocation of resources based on surveys of service suppliers and of unmet need.

(Paterson 1990)

The need for such planning to be accompanied by the development of models of need assessment was raised at a conference of the Lord Chancellor's Legal Aid Advisory Committee on franchising in September 1989, where Kim Economides presented a paper urging that:

In developing regional and national plans for legal aid outlets the Board could usefully explore the application of geographical models which have been used to determine optimum locations for other services . . . For rural areas it is necessary to formulate standards not simply in terms of the quality of work produced by individual firms; one must also consider the availability and range of legal services on offer from firms and other advice agencies. In this sense quantitative and qualitative criteria of adequate provision can be seen to converge.

(Economides 1989)

The need to pull together quantitative and qualitative criteria in developing plans and priorities was identified by Economides in respect of rural areas but applies to all areas as 'the scope, nature and complexity of problems presented in rural areas is not significantly different from that encountered elsewhere' (Elliot 1984).

Conclusion

The next decade will see dramatic changes in the development of publicly funded legal services. The driving force will be twofold: the need to halt the rate of growth in legal aid expenditure; and the growing acceptance that the traditional methods of delivery have not necessarily been the most appropriate to deliver effective access to good legal provision in all areas of law. The need for some major changes in the structure that delivers publicly funded legal services so as to recognize the actual needs for those services was expressed by Goriely:

New tasks require a new service with different priorities and different delivery systems. Much greater emphasis must now be placed on social rights – an area which private practice has traditionally ignored. In the early 70s, this was seen as an area for pioneering group work and test cases. Now, there is also a demand for mass casework in these fields. Nor can we continue the old distinctions between 'lawyers [*sic*] work' and 'lay work'. As the Legal Action Group has stressed, legal services policy must include an information strategy and lay advice agencies.

(Legal Action Group 1992; Goriely 1993)

The challenge is to halt the rate of growth of expenditure whilst preserving and even enhancing access. This will require a focus on those priority areas of law that should be supported by a publicly funded legal provision and by adopting an holistic approach to that provision. The models provide a valuable source of information to assist in that process.

Acknowledgement

A substantial debt of gratitude is owed to Allison McGarrity from the Legal Aid Board's Secretariat who made (and is still making) a substantial contribution to the development of the models guided by my colleagues who were members of the Access Committee of the Board which I chaired (Dianna Beale, David Sinker and Peter Soar). Responsibility for the content and views expressed in this chapter remains entirely with me.

References

Abel, R.L. (1988) *The Legal Profession in England and Wales*. Oxford: Blackwell.

Baldwin, J. and Hill, S. (1988) *The Operation of the Green Form Scheme in England and Wales*. London: Lord Chancellor's Department.

Berthoud, R. and Kempson, E. (1992) *Credit and Debt, The PSI Report*. London: Policy Studies Institute.

Blake, A., Bridges, L. and Cape, E. (1988) *The Duty Solicitor's Handbook*. London: Legal Action Group.

Blake, A. (1993) The franchising opportunity, *Solicitors' Journal*, 137: 886.

Blake, A. and Orchard, S. (1989) Franchising: The next steps, *Law Society's Gazette*, 46: 12.

Blake, A. and Orchard, S. (1990) Franchising: A way forward for advice agencies, *Adviser*: 17.

Cappelletti, M., Gordley, J. and Johnson, E. (1975) *Towards Equal Justice*. New York: Dobbsferry, Oceana.

Cappelletti, M. and Gordley, S. (1977) Legal aid: Modern themes and variations, *Stanford Law Review*, 24: 347.

Economides, K. (1989) 'Franchising and rural legal services', unpublished conference paper, Legal Aid Advisory Committee Legal Services Conference, London, 12 September.

Economides, K. and Blacksell, M. (1987) Access to justice in rural Britain: The final report, *Anglo-American Law Review*, 16: 353.

Elliot, D.K. (1984) *Rural Rights, The Report of the Northumberland Rural Citizens Advice Bureau Experiment*. London: National Association of Citizens' Advice Bureaux.

Goriely, T. (1993) 'Legal aid and the welfare state', unpublished Socio-Legal Studies Association Conference Paper, Exeter, March.

Hinton,T. and Berthoud, R. (1988) *Money Advice Services*. London: Policy Studies Institute.

Hodgson, J.S. (1991) 'Non-duty solicitor attendances at the police station', unpublished report for the Legal Aid Board.

Jarman, B. (1983) Identification of underprivileged areas', *British Medical Journal*, 286: 1705.

Jarman, B. (1984) Underprivileged areas: validation and distribution of scores, *British Medical Journal*, 289: 1587.

Kempson, E. (1989) *Legal Advice and Assistance*. London: Policy Studies Institute.

Legal Action Group (1992) *A Strategy For Justice*. London: Legal Action Group.

Legal Aid Board (1989) *Report to the Lord Chancellor*, Cm 688. London: HMSO.

Legal Aid Board (1990–1) *Annual Reports*, HC 513. London: HMSO.

Legal Aid Board (1991–2) *Annual Reports*, HC 50. London: HMSO.

Legal Aid Board (1992) *Franchising: Next Steps*. London: Legal Aid Board.

Legal Aid Board (1993) *Franchising Specification*. London: Legal Aid Board.

Legal Aid Board (1994–5) *Annual Reports*, HC526. London: HMSO.

Lord Chancellor's Department (1995) *Legal Aid: Targeting Need. The Future of Publicly Funded Help in Solving Legal Problems and Disputes in England and Wales*, Cd. 2854. London: HMSO.

Lord Chancellor's Department (1987) *Legal Aid in England and Wales: A New Framework*, Cm 118. London: HMSO.

Paterson, A. (1990) 'Financing legal services', unpublished report for the Scottish Department.

Rushcliffe Committee (1945) *Report of the Committee on Legal Aid and Legal Advice in England and Wales*, Cmd 6641. London: HMSO.

Sanders, A., Bridges, L., Maloney, A. and Crozier, G. (1989), *Advice and Assistance at Police Stations and the 24 Hour Duty Solicitor Scheme, A Report to the Lord Chancellor*. London: Lord Chancellor's Department.

36th Annual Reports of the Law Society and the Lord Chancellor's Advisory Committee (1985–6) HC87. London: HMSO.

ASSESSING LABOUR MARKET AND TRAINING NEEDS

Introduction

This chapter examines how labour market and training needs are currently assessed and how, ideally, they should be assessed. It begins by outlining the importance of such assessments in labour market and training policy and service delivery. In particular it draws attention to the (rhetoric or substance depending on one's view) increasing emphasis on meeting needs in government policy.

The chapter then provides a skeletal framework within which a labour market and training needs assessment could be undertaken, focusing on its desirable characteristics, objectives and basic components and its linkage to the wider policy process. It then goes on to review existing methods which are used in actually existing assessments in order to draw out some of the relevant issues and problems which confront those seeking to conduct them. Finally it provides some illustrations as to the ways in which labour market and training needs assessments could be made more effective.

Why assess labour market and training needs?

As in all areas of public policy, either implicitly or explicitly, meeting needs is the objective of policy. It follows therefore, that the assessment of needs is a *sine qua non* of the labour market and training policy process. Such an assessment enables the key elements of the policy process to be undertaken (see Campbell 1992; Hawtin *et al.* 1994). These include:

- the identification, definition and specification of 'target' groups or communities who are to be the 'object' or focus of policy, e.g. long term unemployed; lone parents; a peripheral estate;

- the articulation of the nature of the problems and barriers they face in securing their needs;
- the identification of deficiencies in current policies and services which seek to meet these needs;
- the development of strategies, policies and actions to tackle the problems, e.g. customized and accredited training;
- the construction of monitoring and evaluation frameworks, and the establishment of current baselines, to assess progress and the effectiveness of public policies.

Moreover a needs assessment provides an *explicit* recognition that policy is designed to meet need and that policies are to be assessed in terms of the extent to which these needs are met (Percy-Smith 1992).

There are, in addition to this 'normative' case for assessing labour market and training needs as a valuable input to the policy process, a number of concrete and practical reasons why needs assessment is becoming of increasing importance in this field. The labour market, institutional environment and policy context have all been subject to enormous change in recent years. The changing pattern of global competition, industrial restructuring and technological development have engendered profound changes in the occupational structure, skill mix, gender composition, and pattern of employment status within the labour market (see, for example, Barrell 1994; OECD 1994). Labour and training/education markets do not respond very quickly or effectively to such demand-side changes. Because of the need to 'upskill' the labour force to compete effectively (Sturm 1993; Campbell 1994a), it is desirable to identify how both employer and individual needs are changing in relation to their respective requirements for appropriate volumes and levels of labour resources (in the case of employers) and appropriate job opportunities and remuneration (in the case of individuals). Without an understanding of these changing needs, major shifts in the nature of labour demand and supply can generate both inefficiencies and inequalities in the labour market. For example, both structural unemployment and skill shortages can easily coexist because markets have failed to signal effectively either employer or individual needs to each other or they have failed to respond to such signals because of barriers to so doing. Hence their respective needs require articulation through research.

The institutional and policy context have also changed considerably. Extensive legislation on education, training and the labour market (for example Employment Department 1988, 1992; Department for Education 1994) has led to, amongst other things, the continuing reform of vocational education and training; the establishment of training and enterprise councils (TEC); and increased labour market flexibility, changes which demand a clear articulation of the needs of labour market actors, especially in relation to training, so that new institutions, and institutions with a modified status and focus, can adapt and change to meet their new requirements.

Indeed, much recent legislation together with a variety of policy initiatives have explicitly focused on the identification and meeting of needs as the central concern of policy. For example, the White Paper which led to the establishment of TECs made it clear that they were to meet the needs of the local labour market (Employment Department 1988): 'TECs will enable training . . . to be tailored to local needs'. Moreover they were, and are, required to 'examine the local labour market, assessing key skill needs'. It is interesting to note, however, that these needs are essentially defined in terms of *employer* needs: 'There must be a careful assessment of the labour market . . . to identify . . . the skills that must be developed to meet future employer demands'. Locally based training should be 'attuned to the shifting pattern of employer needs' (Employment Department 1988).

A more recent White Paper (Employment Department 1992) focused on increasing employer investment in training, persuading individuals that training pays and ensuring that training providers meet the needs of individuals and employers. It also placed considerable emphasis on developing choice and both individual and employer responsibility for increasing training. This market oriented approach requires the provision of information on employer and individual needs, so that each side of the labour market can adjust their behaviour and so that training providers can identify their 'customer' needs. Such a demand-led approach requires that the volume and structure of provision should be determined by current, emergent and expected labour market needs as indicated by employers and individuals. Moreover, such a market focus requires agencies to meet needs effectively, as specified by the actors themselves, to ensure business survival and development. It also requires the development of intermediaries to acquire, provide and disseminate information on needs, e.g. Gateways to Learning and a reformed Careers Service. Indeed, the prospectus for the provision of Careers Services (Employment Department 1995a) focuses on the provision of information, advice and guidance to help individuals make informed decisions and proposes that plans should be 'underpinned by a clear rationale consistent with assessed local needs'. It goes so far as to specify a clear criterion against which bids will be assessed, namely, 'the extent to which longer term strategy and delivery . . . are based on an assessment of local and client needs'.

The White Paper on competitiveness also makes it clear that meeting labour market needs is vital not only to improve the functioning of the labour market and to increase the skills of the labour force, but to increase economic competitiveness (HM Government 1994a). The government's strategic guidance to TECs (HM Government 1994b), whose focus is now wider than labour market and training needs, requires TEC Corporate Plans to show 'the economic development and regeneration needs of the locality . . . and what TEC and other partners plan to do to meet those needs' and to 'identify local skill needs'.

All these developments identify the assessment of labour market and training needs as vital to a variety of parts of the policy process and to specific aspects of, and groups, in the labour market. Others have also shown how assessing the needs of different groups in the labour market is a valuable tool in policy development (for example Pitcher 1994, on ethnic minorities; and TEC National Council 1994 on equal opportunities more generally). Even the most market oriented approaches to policy, in so far as they focus on quality, require a focus on the identification of customer needs and how these can best be satisfied. Consequently they require a needs assessment, albeit one which specifies needs in a particular fashion.

Moreover, agencies charged with the responsibility to deliver or manage *services* designed to meet needs require their clear identification. This involves a strong focus on understanding the barriers that stand between individuals and improved labour market participation and access to education and training, and the problems that employers face in acquiring and developing the labour resources they require. The very existence of these problems are evidence of 'market failure' and hence a means of assessment of their needs is required – an assessment which would not be required if markets led to outcomes which satisfied both individuals and employers. The existence of skill shortages, recruitment difficulties, structural unemployment and skill deficits are, at one and the same time, indicators of such market failure and a case for effective needs assessment.

A framework for assessing labour market and training needs

It is one thing to develop policies or services based on, and addressed at, meeting needs; it is another to actually identify the needs. Whose needs? Their needs for what? In this section we address a number of the conceptual issues in assessing labour market and training needs by outlining a possible framework or set of characteristics, which might provide a basis for an effective labour market and training needs assessment 'system'. In other words we begin to articulate what should ideally be included in a comprehensive system which could be used as a basis for meeting the needs identified in the previous section.

We can identify nine such characteristics:

1 responsive – to user requirements;
2 accessible – available to, and understandable by, different user groups;
3 economical – where the benefits achieved outweigh the costs involved and where clear priorities are identified in relation to resource constraints;
4 timely – with agreed frequencies consistent with user needs providing regular and up-to-date information;
5 reliable – statistically robust;
6 comprehensive – reflecting the needs of all the user groups;
7 consistent – where definitions, classifications and thus information is comparable over time;
8 flexible – so as to be capable of amendment in the light of new requirements;
9 systematic – coherent and coordinated.

In terms of *objectives*, a framework for assessing labour market and training needs should seek to meet the requirements for four different user groups. The first group are *policy makers* at local, regional and national level who require it for strategy, policy, setting objectives/targets and monitoring and evaluation. The second group are *employers* – to improve their knowledge of the changing nature of the labour force to help them respond effectively to change in terms

Figure 9.1 Components of a labour market and training needs assessment system

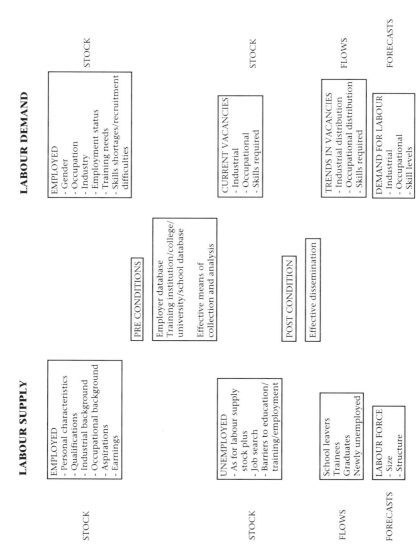

LABOUR SUPPLY

EMPLOYED
- Personal characteristics
- Qualifications
- Industrial background
- Occupational background
- Aspirations
- Earnings

STOCK

UNEMPLOYED
- As for labour supply
  stock plus
- Job search
- Barriers to education/
  training/employment

STOCK

School leavers
Trainees
Graduates
Newly unemployed

FLOWS

LABOUR FORCE
- Size
- Structure

FORECASTS

PRE CONDITIONS

Employer database
Training institution/college/
university/school database

Effective means of
collection and analysis

POST CONDITION

Effective dissemination

LABOUR DEMAND

EMPLOYED
- Gender
- Occupation
- Industry
- Employment status
- Training needs
- Skills shortages/recruitment
  difficulties

STOCK

CURRENT VACANCIES
- Industrial
- Occupational
- Skills required

STOCK

TRENDS IN VACANCIES
- Industrial distribution
- Occupational distribution
- Skills required

FLOWS

DEMAND FOR LABOUR
- Industrial
- Occupational
- Skill levels

FORECASTS

of recruitment practices and terms/conditions of work; proactively identify potential skill shortages; and identify possible future training needs. The third group consists of *education and training institutions* who require information to help them develop their corporate plans; estimate the demand for education and training of different types; and adjust course provision in the light of changing demand patterns. Fourth, *individuals* need information to help them make decisions about future education and training activities as well as job search and career development decisions.

This could lead to the generation of the following broad components of such a labour market and training needs assessment system (LMTNAS) as outlined in Figure 9.1. There are four main elements of such a system. First, several *preconditions* need to be in place to enable the relevant information to be collectable and capable of appropriate analysis. Second, the *results* of the assessment must be effectively disseminated to users. Third, the information must relate to both the *demand* and *supply* sides of the labour market. Fourth, information must be collected on both *stocks* and *flows* and attempts must be made to assess *future* trends.

The precise configuration of the information, the priorities, the modes and detail of the analysis will depend also on the implicit or explicit theoretical approach that the labour market agency(ies) adopts, whether because of its ideological stance, aims and values or because of the advice and experience of its professional practitioners (Campbell 1992). The *interpretation* of information is a key aspect of needs assessment. Because facts do not speak for themselves, the final identification of needs requires analytical skills and the linkage of such research results to the clear identification, specification and assessment of problems and the formulation of appropriate policy objectives.

Indeed the assessment should also provide much of the necessary resources to design strategy, policies and action plans, as well as the subsequent monitoring and evaluation of actions and consequent adjustment to such strategies, objectives, policies and action plans in the light of findings. In this way needs assessment has an important role to play at each stage of the labour market policy process (see Figure 9.2). (More detail can be found in Campbell 1992.)

The final point before turning to a consideration of the methods that are available for obtaining the information required for a LMTNA is to reflect on the implicit/explicit definition of needs to be used in this framework. In principle it is possible in many cases to incorporate normative, felt and comparative needs (see Bradshaw 1972) or at least to address each of them separately. In practice, because many assessments rely heavily on official statistical data, the main approach tends to be comparative – local relative to national positions; actual versus target conditions; or actual versus explicit standards in relation to a reference group (e.g. a disadvantaged group relative to the population as a whole).

However, where primary research is conducted (and this occurs particularly at a local level, especially in TECs) or in relation to specific groups (e.g. the disabled or employers) and on specific policy issues (e.g. individual commitment) at a national level, the main focus is *felt* need. In these cases the views of individuals and/or employers are identified (e.g. in identifying the barriers to

Figure 9.2 Needs assessment and the labour market policy process

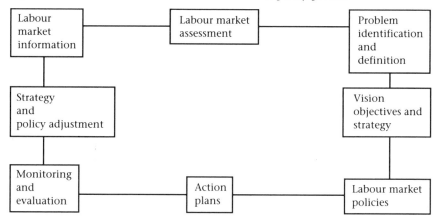

training participation or in identifying skill shortages). Rarely is normative need the criterion, except in so far as professionals and experts, in the form of civil servants, consultants, researchers, agency actors and executives, or politicians, interpret the results in a particular way. Because such interpretation is an essential element in any effective LMTNA it is clear that comparative or felt needs are subsequently *mediated* through a normative lens. Rarely however, are the needs assessments or definitions explicit. Hence the approach is more layered and less coherent than that ideally required (Percy-Smith 1992). There is, therefore, no clear answer without further detailed research to the question of how ultimately needs are defined in this field. Finally, we can note that the valuable work on theories of human need and approaches to identifying and measuring 'intermediate needs' is too aggregative for our purposes of assessing labour market and training needs (Doyal and Gough 1991).

Methods: Issues and problems

We now turn to a consideration of the methods that are available for obtaining the information required to undertake a LMTNA. As has been often pointed out (Haughton 1992; Hawtin *et al.* 1994), much work on labour market and training needs, especially at the national level, relies on existing data and its analysis (so-called 'secondary' data) rather than data specially collected to assess such needs (so-called 'primary' data). Moreover, as we have seen, information should ideally be collected both on the needs of the target group or locality *and* on existing provision/services. Ideally, also, we should have available information on best practice and alternative strategies and policies, if the LMTNA is to be comprehensive and utilized in relation to all stages of the policy process. In terms of sources, the different aspects of needs should be covered, so that information is available on felt, normative and comparative needs, thus necessitating the collection of information from the target group(s) themselves, 'experts', and from secondary data sources which provide an element of comparability across groups or areas. A LMTNA should also involve the use of a mechanism to attempt to reconcile divergences in the results emanating from these different sources, so as to reach more of a consensus on the specification of needs and what is to be done.

In practice, such an approach is in its infancy. Because of a limited understanding of the needs assessment process, severe resource constraints, political and policy constraints, tight timescales, or the restricted policy focus of the responsible agency, needs assessments are currently partial with respect to most or all of the issues outlined above.

In many cases *secondary* data is the dominant or sole source of information. The sources of such data are usefully summarized in Healey (1991) and Haughton (1992). At the *national* level these sources are generally comprehensive and offer a highly valuable information framework. Most of the information is available through NOMIS (the National Online Manpower Information System) in particular the Census of Employment, Population Census, Labour Force Survey and data on unemployment and vacancies. The NOMIS system is ably summarized by Blackmore and Townsend (in Healey 1991). Whilst accessible and an extremely useful starting point, it does however suffer from some serious limitations. First, it is only as good as the data set that it uses (see below). Second, whilst regional and local information is available via NOMIS, again there are severe constraints on its use as a result of the data sets themselves. Third, it does not cover some critical issues at all, most notably, changing skill levels and skill shortages.

Critically the data sources themselves are limited. For example with regard to the Labour Force Survey, whilst it is the most useful and comprehensive 'supply side' information source (it covers employment by occupation and industry, employment status and training in a good deal of detail) the sample size does not allow it to be used successfully at a local level, especially if we need to focus on a particular subgroup. Unemployment and vacancy data are also limited. For example, in the former case it is a by-product of the benefit system. Consequently, changes in benefit rules alter the size and composition of the unemployed, making time series analysis extremely hazardous, and, in any case, the data set does not necessarily represent those seeking employment. Recent changes with regard to invalidity benefit and, most notably, the Job Seekers allowance, further complicate the picture. With regard to vacancies, this information only covers those registered at job centres and, as there is no compulsory regulation of such vacancies, the data set covers, at most, only a third of all vacancies and indeed a highly skewed cross-section of them.

Other data sets are also limited. For example, the otherwise extremely useful Census of Employment is only undertaken every two years and the results usually take a further two years to be published. From 1995, however, this census (which in fact in most years is actually a sample!) will be replaced with an annual survey of employment, with results being published much more quickly.

The main problems attached to such data sources, however, relate to the local level, where most needs assessment is required, for example by TECs, the Careers Service, Employment Service, local authorities, development agencies and so on. The data is either not collected, not available or is insufficiently robust. The data also rarely allows one to get 'underneath' the problem being examined. Not only is it often difficult to undertake much analysis of the information, both within, and especially between, data sets as the individual records are not available, but also questions that need answering are not asked in the original surveys on which the data is based.

To meet this requirement one needs primary data collection and analysis, based on the particular requirements for the relevant needs assessment. At the national level a wide range of surveys and research are indeed undertaken, most often commissioned by the Employment Department, precisely to provide more detailed information on the basis of which needs can be more effectively assessed. For example, the annual Skills Monitoring Survey of employers assesses employers' skill needs, albeit based on hard to fill vacancies as a measure of skill needs, a measure shown to be less than entirely appropriate (Baldwin and Campbell 1993). The results are published annually (see, for example, IFF 1995). Similarly the quarterly survey of the Confederation of British Industry (CBI) and the British Chambers of Commerce (BCC) provide useful insights into skill shortages and some other aspects of labour market needs at national and regional levels. Information is also available for specific groups in the labour market. For example, the Youth Cohort Study provides extensive detail of the behaviour and decisions of 16–19 year-olds as they progress through education, training and the labour market. Adult Literacy and Basic Skills Unit (ALBSU) provides a regular survey of adult literacy to identify explicitly the needs of those with literacy and numeracy deficiencies. Most of these national studies are summarized in the useful annual Labour Market and Skill Trends (see, for example, Employment Department 1995b).

At local level the main means by which information on labour market and training needs can be obtained is through a skills audit. Ideally this should obtain information on the supply of, demand for, and creation of skills, through education and training (Haughton 1992). In practice most are strongly supply side oriented, obtaining information on personal characteristics, qualifications, informal skills, work histories, barriers to education/training and labour market progression and so on. Haughton (1991) reviews 14 skills audits and concludes that the 'critical success factors' in undertaking such work include the involvement of the local community; the link to concrete policy/practice recommendations; and effective dissemination of results. We would add to this the need to ensure audits are linked to actions and thus real outcomes, a condition which requires their linkage to resource availability and policy formulation.

However many local studies are also undertaken of employers' needs. Until recently TECs were under a contractual obligation to the Employment Department to collect such information, through for example, the CALLMI system. Whilst this is no longer the case, many do undertake or commission useful, detailed surveys.

There are, however, serious remaining methodological problems in the existing information base which restricts our ability to undertake an effective LMTNA particularly at a local level. Many of these problems will be evident from a comparison of the brief review of methods outlined in this section of the chapter and the characteristics of an effective framework outlined in the previous section of the chapter. First, the information is piecemeal, un-coordinated and not systematized. Second, the same (core) information is not available in all localities, making comparative work almost impossible in many cases. Third, the data sets are not always available to all the main local actors and policy makers – a deficiency which effective data pooling could usefully address. Fourth, whilst much information is collected for particular uses it is rarely integrated with that which is collected for other uses, and even more rarely subjected to subsequent analysis. Finally, much of the information relates to *current* labour market and training issues. What is required is a much more concerted examination of trends over time, a better understanding of the processes generated by changing needs, and, especially, an attempt to forecast future labour market and training needs (individual and employer). In a practi-cal policy and action sense, it will take providers time to adapt to identified needs. Moreover, it would be highly desirable for there to be a national frame-work for effective information collection for labour market and training needs to allow such an approach to be developed and in consequence allow a more systematic and coherent identification of needs.

Towards more effective labour market and training needs assessments (LMTNAs)

Despite there being both a powerful case for undertaking systematic LMTNAs and despite policy makers appearing to recognize the importance of ensuring that policy and provision should seek to meet these needs, LMTNAs are in their infancy. At a national level there have been some useful needs assessments of particular groups, most notably a number which related to disabled people (for example, Lakey and Simpkins 1994). These generally arise when the objectives of the assessment are clear and needs-based. For example, the Policy Studies Institute study aimed to 'identify issues of policy importance in the field of employment rehabilitation for the disabled . . . identify ways local provision should be developed to meet the needs of all clients' (Lakey and Simpkins 1994).

We should also draw attention to a valuable, though now dated, explicit examination of needs assessment in relation to post-16 education, which offers perhaps the most sophisticated needs assessment at a national level that has yet been attempted (Packwood and Whitaker 1988). This study includes a rigorous and systematic attempt to identify needs in a manner consistent with the approach advocated in this book. It also develops a sound framework for needs assessment, undertakes such an assessment and identifies what is required to develop needs assessments more effectively in the future. It neatly summarizes the key characteristics of what remain the differences between contemporary practice and what they call an 'objective led' approach to needs assessment (see Figure 9.3).

Whilst current approaches are characterized by existing relations, interests, client needs, provision and work processes, they should rather be characterized

Figure 9.3 Needs assessment in theory and practice

Theory	Practice
Proactive	Conservative
Rational	Reactive
Elitist	Incremental
Centralized	Pluralistic
Purposive	Professionally dominated
Conflictual	Negotiative

Source: Adapted from Packwood and Whitaker (1988) Tables 4 and 12

by the objectives of policy makers who should decide whose needs are assessed and/or prioritized. Whilst such an approach is potentially less participative and democratic than that espoused in this book, it nonetheless indicates how little, in some ways, needs assessment has developed in the field of labour markets and training in recent years.

At a local level there is insufficient knowledge and recognition of practices in different localities. There is no appropriate framework, network or set of incentives to encourage the development and dissemination of good practice in LMTNAs, though, for a time the Employment Department did produce a series of, often very useful, good practice guides for TECs (see, for example, Employment Department undated). The Employment Department's Skills and Enterprise Network does however provide useful information and a potential vehicle for future development in this area. For those readers who are interested, we believe our own approach to supply side and demand side data offers useful lessons (see, for example, Percy-Smith *et al.* 1993 and Baldwin *et al.* 1995 on the former; and Baldwin and Campbell 1993 on the latter).

The main way in which labour market and training needs are assessed at a local level in a systematic way is through the annual Labour Market Assessments (now called Economic Assessments) that TECs increasingly undertake with their local partners. It is these documents which are supposed to identify local labour market and training needs. Based on the secondary and primary information discussed above we believe that they offer the best opportunity for developing a systematic and coherent approach to LMTNAs in the near future. We have examined a large number of these assessments and we outline here the main ways in which they need to be developed to secure a sound basis for the assessment of local labour market and training needs (Campbell 1994b). First, they need to be linked much more clearly to the TECs' own corporate plans, the plans of other relevant agencies (for example colleges and the Employment Service) and the local area's economic development strategy. Currently this linkage is insufficiently clear or detailed. Second, assessments need to be more analytical. They require an explicit definition, identification and measurement of needs; an explicit assessment of current policies and provision in the light of that need; and a clear identification of the service or policy gaps that exist. Third, they need to be more oriented to the future on both supply and demand sides. Fourth, they need to incorporate explicitly (as several do already) the 'felt' needs of individuals; reflect their priorities; and be inclusive of, particularly, those at risk of labour market and skills exclusion. Fifth, assessments need to identify a coherent framework for assessing labour market and training needs (compare the framework proposed earlier in this chapter) preferably on a national basis with the TEC National Council and/or Employment Department.

Indeed the Employment Department's good practice guide has argued that the focus of such TEC assessments should be to provide

> a thorough assessment of current and future needs of businesses and individuals . . . to . . . assess the adequacy of current provision; consider how it should develop to cater for enlarging needs . . . and generate baselines against which policies can be evaluated.
>
> (Employment Department undated)

We are still some way from achieving this goal.

Conclusion

We have seen that a labour market and training needs assessment, or LMTNA, can make a major contribution to each stage of the policy process. Its ultimate purpose is to ensure that strategy, policy and provision is determined as far as possible by needs. To this end a LMTNA needs to be seen as integral to the policy and planning process at the national, regional and local levels. The Employment Department, government offices for the regions, TECs and their partners should require that a LMTNA be undertaken at national, regional and local levels respectively. The government's proposal to undertake a national skills audit may be a valuable step in this direction.

Needs assessment is increasingly necessary, because of major labour market policy and institutional changes and because of both explicit and implicit policy focuses on meeting people's needs. However a number of issues need to be addressed to ensure that LMTNAs can play an effective role in public policy.

Whose needs are to be assessed? Whilst it is clear that both employers' and individuals' needs are vital, important issues arise to the extent that there is a mismatch between these needs. It is also important to ensure that the needs assessment should include those who are not currently the target of policy or recipients of service, so as to ensure the inclusion of all those currently or potentially active in the labour market. If priorities in LMTNAs have to be identified in advance then perhaps the focus should be on those who face barriers to their full labour market integration and in those policy areas where there is evidence of 'market failure'.

There needs to be a more consistent and coherent approach to collecting and examining the primary information required to undertake LMTNAs. The results also need to be linked more effectively to the wider policy and planning process within responsible organizations.

User/client involvement needs to be enhanced. Our own extensive experience and the results of research (for example, Geroy and Wright 1993; Mosely and Heaney 1993) demonstrate that we need to go beyond surveying individuals and employers about their needs, towards consulting them or even involving them. 'Ownership' and a sense of policy makers and providers being in touch with local needs is increasingly important. This has implications for how the information required for LMTNAs is collected, in terms, for example, of the use of focus groups and panels, and the dissemination of the results of needs assessments, and indeed for the involvement of clients/users in policy and service delivery.

The technical capacity to undertake effective LMTNAs also requires further development. Currently there is extensive use of consultants and researchers in the field. This gives rise, on occasion, to 'ownership' problems and also assumes that the external consultants have a substantive understanding of needs assessments, which is not always the case. The use of external agencies should also involve a strong element of 'know-how transfer' to the client, so that skills and capacities can be developed in-house.

There is also, in many cases, a tendency to treat employers, and especially individuals, in LMTNAs as consumers or users of services rather than as citizens, in the sense of failing to involve them in policy/service development. Indeed sometimes they are treated solely as research 'subjects', asked their views or to provide information but not involved further in the assessment, let alone the policy process flowing from it.

Local labour market assessments have great potential to develop effective LMTNAs but do require a more explicit needs focus and interpretation. Perhaps we require a formal needs review mechanism for labour market and training agencies (e.g. TECs, colleges, careers services) where an annual 'needs statement' could be produced which would be used as a basis for policy review and development (cf. Packwood and Whitaker 1988).

References

Baldwin, S. and Campbell, M. (1993) Recruitment difficulties and skills shortages, *Regional Studies*, 27(3): 270–9.

Baldwin, S. *et al.* (1995) *Yorkshire and Humberside Skills and Training Survey*. Leeds: Policy Research Unit.

Barrell, R. (ed.) (1994) *The UK Labour Market: Comparative Aspects and Institutional Approaches*. Cambridge: Cambridge University Press.

Bradshaw, J. (1972) The concept of need, *New Society*, 30 March: 640–3.

Campbell, M. (1992) A strategic approach to the local labour market. In M. Campbell and K. Duffy (eds) *Local Labour Markets: Problems and Policies*. Harlow: Longman.

Campbell, M. (1994a) *Education, Training and Economic Performance*. Leeds: Policy Research Unit.

Campbell, M. (1994b) From labour market to economic assessments, paper to LEPU Seminar, London: October 14.

Department for Education (1994) *Education and Training for the 21st Century*, Cm 1536. London: HMSO.

Doyal, L. and Gough, I. (1991) *A Theory of Human Need*. London: Macmillan.

Employment Department (1988) *Employment for the 1990s*, Cm 540. London: HMSO.

Employment Department (1992) *People, Jobs and Opportunity*, Cm 1810. London: HMSO.

Employment Department (1995a) *Prospectus for the Provision of Careers Services*. London: HMSO.

Employment Department (1995b) *Labour Market and Skill Trends*. London, Employment Department.

Employment Department (undated) *Developing Good Practice: Producing a Labour Market Assessment*. London: HMSO.

Geroy, G. and Wright, P. (1993) Using skill needs assessment in support of economic development strategy, *Journal of European Industrial Training*, 17(9): 2–24.

Haughton, G. (1991) In search of a moving target: Skills surveys and audits, *Local Economy*, 6(2): 177–83.

Haughton, G. (1992) Analysing the labour market. In M. Campbell and K. Duffy (eds) *Local Labour Markets: Problems and Policies*. Harlow: Longman.

Hawtin, M., Hughes, G. and Percy-Smith, J. (1994) *Community Profiling*. Buckingham: Open University Press.

Healey, M. (1991) *Economic Activity and Land Use: The Changing Information Base*. Harlow: Longman.

HM Government (1994a) *Competitiveness: Helping Business Win*. London: HMSO.

HM Government (1994b) *TECs: Towards 2000. The Government's Strategic Guidance to TECs*. London: HMSO.

IFF Research Ltd (1995) *Skill Needs in Britain*. London: IFF.

Lakey, J. and Simpkins, R. (1994) *Employment Rehabilitation for Disabled People*. London: Policy Studies Institute.

Mosely, J. and Heaney, M. (1993) Needs assessment across disciplines, *Performance Improvement Quarterly*, 7(1): 60–79.

OECD (1994) *The OECD Jobs Study*. Paris: OECD.

Packwood, T. and Whitaker, T. (1988) *Needs Assessment in Post 16 Education*. London: Falmer Press.

Percy-Smith, J. (1992) Auditing social needs, *Policy and Politics*, 20(1): 29–34.

Percy-Smith, J. (1993) *People, Jobs and Training in Wirral City Lands*. Leeds: Policy Research Unit.

Pitcher, J. (1994) TECs and local communities: The role of research in a multi-ethnic district, *Local Economy*, 9(1): 62–72.

Sturm, R. (1993) *How Do Education and Training Affect a Country's Economic Performance?* Santa Monica, CA: Rand Institute on Education and Training.

TEC National Council (1994) *Equal Opportunities and Special Training Needs: A National Framework for Action by TECs*. London: TEC National Council.

CONCLUSION: THEMES AND ISSUES

The aim of this concluding chapter is to identify some themes and issues which have emerged from the case study chapters. These relate to the contexts within which needs assessments are being developed and used; theoretical and conceptual issues; methods and methodologies; and the impact of needs assessments on both citizens and policy.

Need is a key justification for the existence of public services. It is also part of the common sense language of public provision. This remains the case despite arguments against the usefulness, validity and acceptability of the concept of need from a variety of different sources over a number of years. Indeed, the concept of need is currently undergoing something of a revival in academic debate and in debates about social justice and the future of the welfare state. In many of these discussions needs are seen as forming the basis for a set of enforceable social and economic rights.

However need is not just reappearing as a legitimate concept in academic circles. As the case study chapters have shown, at a policy level too, there has been an increasing emphasis on meeting need as one criterion of effectiveness. It is interesting to note how this emphasis has, in part, arisen out of the 'new managerialism' evident in many public sector organizations. This concept has several strands to it, including an increasing concern to demonstrate that public funds are spent in ways that really make a difference and an attempt to move away from what were seen as producer-led services to needs-based services. However, despite a broadly similar context, the way in which needs have been and are being used in relation to public services differs markedly across policy areas and organizations, as the case study chapters have demonstrated. Some common themes can, nevertheless, be identified.

First, there is little evidence of a well thought out, coherent theory of need informing policy development. There is certainly no general, overarching theory of need within which needs in relation to particular services or issues can be located. Without such an overarching theory it is almost inevitable that needs will continue to be defined in relation to the availability of existing services rather than an agreed optimum or even minimum standard.

Second, the status of the needs identified through the various assessment procedures is often not clear. In most cases an identification of need brings with it no clear right to services of a particular kind to meet that need. This is especially the case where needs are met, wholly or in part, through the market (e.g. housing) or within cash limited budgets (e.g. the Social Fund). It is also true where an identified need is then subject to further scrutiny to establish whether it meets certain *eligibility* criteria (e.g. community care).

The range of different methods and techniques used in assessing needs reflects, in part, the lack of consensus about what needs are and their status in relation to policy. Because there is a lack of clarity about what constitutes need in any given context it is not clear what should be assessed, nor how that assessment should be conducted. One contentious issue is the extent to which citizens, as opposed to 'experts' or professionals, should be involved in the assessment of their own needs. However, it is interesting to note that there appears to be something of a trend in favour of citizen involvement and that this is often linked to strategies for citizen empowerment. The extent to which citizen participation in needs assessment is, in reality, currently an empowering process must be open to serious question.

Nevertheless the concern to involve citizens has resulted in the development of a number of innovatory, often qualitative, research methods to complement more traditional methods of secondary data analysis and statistical manipulation.

A further issue to emerge from the case study chapters is whether organizations charged with the responsibility for undertaking needs assessments have the necessary skills and expertise to undertake what are increasingly sophisticated pieces of research. This is a particular issue in relation to health needs assessments and assessments of training needs but is an important factor in other areas of policy too. In some cases central government departments have sought to fill this skills gap by providing more or less detailed guidelines on how to undertake needs assessments. As we have already noted, these guidelines are not informed by any overarching theory of need and there is little consistency in approach across government departments or agencies. There is also a tension between on the one hand, producing prescriptive models, which have the advantage of providing the possibility, at least, of more useful and valid data collected in a way that allows comparisons to be made across areas; and, on the other, local discretion and the need to employ assessment techniques that are appropriate to the locality. This was shown to be a particular issue in relation to housing needs assessments and community care assessments. However there may also be more fundamental and important issues at stake here. In the absence of centrally determined models which specify what needs are in relation to particular policy areas and set out optimum or minimum standards of provision in relation to those needs, it is difficult to see how equity between geographical areas can be achieved.

A related point is the need for information and expertise to be pooled both within organizations and between organizations. The importance of this was shown in relation to the sharing of labour market information, but it is of relevance to other areas as well. It is not an effective use of resources for organizations to undertake several separate assessments of need in a particular area. Such an approach is not only not cost-effective but also fails to appreciate the essentially interconnected nature of human needs. A more holistic approach is advocated in the chapter on community needs assessments.

There is widespread recognition across policy areas of the potential benefits that could accrue as a result of needs assessments in terms of the provision of more effective services and policies. However there is some doubt about how far this potential is currently being realized because of some of the issues identified above – lack of clarity about the concept of need; lack of skills and expertise in devising and implementing assessment techniques; and lack of resources devoted to needs assessment. How to incorporate information on needs into the strategic planning and policy development process is another difficult practical issue. Needs assessments are of no benefit in and of themselves; they should be undertaken with clear objectives and should be tied to a commitment to review services and resource allocation in the light of the information which they provide.

Despite perceived benefits in terms of improved information on which to base decision making, there is resistance to the idea on the part of some policy makers who fear that identifying needs will result in raised expectations and increased demands that cannot be met from the shrinking resources available for public services. This is a real issue that has to be confronted and relates to the question, identified above, of the status of needs. In the absence of enforceable social and economic rights, information about the needs of citizens can be 'advisory' only. In other words it *may* be used to determine the pattern of resource allocation but it does not have to be so used. Furthermore we should be careful of needs assessment techniques being used to legitimate a process which results in the targeting of resources on a residual group of people with 'special needs' that cannot be met through the market.

Needs assessments as a basis for public service provision are still in their infancy and, as this book has demonstrated, there are a number of unresolved issues which are limiting their extent and impact. Nevertheless it is clear that, properly conducted, they do have the potential to contribute to more effective public services, more needs being met and, depending on the methods used, the empowerment of citizens and service users.

INDEX

COMMUNITY PROFILING
AUDITING SOCIAL NEEDS

Murray Hawtin, Geraint Hughes, Janie Percy-Smith with Anne Foreman

Social auditing and community profiles are increasingly being used in relation to a number of policy areas, including: housing, community care, community health, urban regeneration and local economic development. *Community Profiling* provides a practical guide to the community profiling process which can be used by professionals involved in the planning and delivery of services, community workers, community organizations, voluntary groups and tenants' associations. In addition it will provide an invaluable step-by-step guide to social science students involved in practical research projects.

The book takes the reader through the community profiling process beginning with consideration of what a community profile is, defining aims and objectives and planning the research. It then looks at a variety of methods for collecting, storing and analysing information and ways of involving the local community. Finally it considers how to present the information and develop appropriate action-plans. The book also includes a comprehensive annotated bibliography of recent community profiles and related literature.

Contents
What is a community profile? – Planning a community profile – Involving the community – Making use of existing information – Collecting new information – Survey methods – Storing and analysing data – Collating and presenting information – Not the end – Annotated bibliography – Index.

208pp   0 335 19113 4 (Paperback)

SOCIAL CARE IN A MIXED ECONOMY

Gerald Wistow, Martin Knapp, Brian Hardy and Caroline Allen

This book describes the mixed economy of community care in England and analyses the efforts and activities of local authorities to promote and develop it. It is based on national documentary and statistical evidence and on more detailed research with twenty-four local authorities; and includes a case study on the transfer of residential homes to the independent sector.

The roles of social services departments have been progressively redefined to emphasize responsibility for creating and managing a mixed economy. This entails a major cultural shift for departments which may be summarized as involving moves from providing to enabling, and from administration to management. It also implies the need for new skills and structures. *Social Care in a Mixed Economy* traces the historical changes; the local interpretations of central government policy; how authorities actually have been developing mixed economies; the main opportunities or incentives for promoting a mixed economy; and the main obstacles to its development.

Contents

176pp   0 335 19043 X (Paperback)   0 335 19044 8 (Hardback)

DELIVERING WELFARE
THE GOVERNANCE OF THE SOCIAL SERVICES IN THE 1990s

Tony Butcher

Recent years have seen a series of radical changes in the arrangements for the delivery of education, housing, health and other major social services. Local authorities are being transformed from front line delivery agencies of the welfare state into enabling authorities. Privatization, marketization and the search for efficiency are now important features of the system of welfare delivery. The Citizen's Charter and other developments reflect a growing concern with consumerism and customer sensitivity.

This book provides an up-to-date survey of the role of central government, local authorities, the health services and other agencies responsible for delivering the social services, and the directions that welfare delivery has taken in recent years. At a time when the organization of welfare delivery and the quality of the public services are high on the political agenda, it provides a timely study of an important subject. It will be of interest to both students and practitioners in social policy, public administration and politics.

Contents
Introduction – Part I: The public face of welfare – Central government and welfare – The government of welfare outside Whitehall – The coordination and planning of welfare – Accountability and the public – Part II: New directions in the delivery of welfare – The rolling back of the local welfare state – The privatization of welfare delivery – The search for efficiency and value for money – The customer orientation – Conclusion – Further reading – References – Index.

208pp   0 335 15710 6 (Paperback)   0 335 15711 4 (Hardback)